WORKBOOK

to accompany

THIRD EDITION

A CANADIAN WRITER'S GUIDE

Jack Finnbogason and Al Valleau

Prepared by
Juanita Simeon and Lazaros Simeon

THOMSON NELSON™

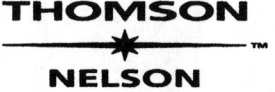

COPYRIGHT © 2005 by Nelson, a division of Thomson Canada Limited. Nelson is a registered trademark used herein under license.

For more information contact Nelson, 1120 Birchmount Road, Scarborough, Ontario M1K 5G4. Or you can visit our Internet site at www.nelson.com.

ALL RIGHTS RESERVED. No part of this work covered by the copyright hereon may be reproduced or used in any form or by any means—graphic, electronic, or mechanical including photocopying, recording, taping, web distribution or information storage and retrieval systems—without the written permission of the publisher.

Contents

Basic Grammar 1
    B1 Identifying Parts of Speech 1
    B2 Identifying Phrases 4
    B2 Constructing Clauses 6
    B2 Identifying Clauses 7

Sentence Elements 9
    S1 Identifying Parts of Sentences 9
    S2 Identifying Sentence Patterns 13
    S3 Identifying Sentence Types 14
    S5 Editing Sentences for Variety 16

Grammatical Sentences 18
    G1 Sentence Fragments 18
    G1 Run-on Sentences 21
    G2 Subject-Verb Agreement 23
    G2 Verb Tense and Mood Agreement 25
    G2 Pronoun-Antecedent Agreement 28
    G3 Unclear Pronoun Reference 30
    G3 Misplaced Modifiers 32
    G3 Dangling Modifiers 34
    G3 Faulty Parallel Structure 36

Usage and Diction 39
    U1 Redundancy and Wordiness 39
    U1 Appropriate Connotations and Slang 43
    U1 Clichés 45
    U1 Idioms 46
    U2 Pronoun Case 47
    U3 Pronoun Choice 48
    U4 Agreement and Collective Nouns 49
    U5 Inclusive Language 50
    U7 Active and Passive Voice 51

Punctuation 53
- P1 The Comma 53
- P2 The Semicolon and the Colon 55
- P3 Review of the Semicolon, the colon, and the Comma 56
- P4 Apostrophes 58
- P5 Other Punctuation Marks 59
- P6 Punctuation Review 60

Mechanics 62
- M2 Capitalization 62
- M3 Abbreviations 63
- M4 Numbers 64
- M5 Hyphens 65

Answers 66

Name _____ Course _____ Date _____

BASIC GRAMMAR

B1. IDENTIFYING PARTS OF SPEECH. If you have problems completing this exercise, refer to pages 39-59 of *A Canadian Writer's Guide*. Answers appear at the end of this workbook.

1. **Underline and identify the nouns, pronouns (excluding possessive pronouns) and verbs in each of the following sentences: 1 = noun, 2 = pronoun, 3 = verb.**

    a. Into every life a little rain must fall.
    b. A picture is worth a thousand words.
    c. Has the cat got your tongue?
    d. A stitch in time saves nine.
    e. After many a summer dies the swan.
    f. Good fences make good neighbours.
    g. A fool and his money are soon parted.
    h. Seeing is believing.
    i. Don't count your chickens before they hatch.
    j. Talk is cheap.

2. **Underline and identify the following five parts of speech: 1 = adjective, 2 = adverb, 3 = conjunction, 4 = preposition, 5 = article.**

    a. A penny saved is a penny earned.
    b. The family that prays together, stays together.
    c. Look before you leap.
    d. When the cat's away, the mice will play.
    e. Live and learn.
    f. You can't judge a book by its cover.
    g. The rain in Spain falls mainly on the plain.
    h. A rolling stone gathers no moss.
    i. Procrastination is the thief of time.
    j. A watched pot never boils.

B1 *Identifying Parts of Speech* **1**

Name _____ Course _____ Date _____

3. **Underline and identify the nouns, pronouns, and verbs in the following sentences: 1 = noun, 2 = pronoun, 3 = verb.**

   a. Business executives spend their lives looking for a good deal.

   b. When you deal the cards, you should be very careful.

   c. The picture in my colouring book was a mass of green and blue.

   d. Picture a beautiful beach with palm trees swaying.

   e. A silk shirt is cooler than one made from synthetic fibre because natural fabrics can breathe.

   f. Silk is far more expensive than cotton.

   g. Manual labour is becoming a thing of the past.

   h. Reading a manual is a trial even for those of us who are keen on technology.

   i. The police officer will book the drunken driver.

   j. Librarians, like me, believe that a book is a precious commodity.

4. **Underline and identify the following five parts of speech: 1 = adjective, 2 = adverb, 3 = conjunction, 4 = preposition, 5 = article.**

   a. A new study reveals that cultural factors influence how dyslexia manifests itself.

   b. Dyslexia is characterized by a greater than normal difficulty in reading and spelling.

   c. This neurological disorder affects the brains of Chinese and English speakers differently.

   d. Previously, it was assumed that dyslexia, even in different languages, had the same biological underpinning.

   e. Many researchers believed the root was located in the left temporal region of the brain.

   f. Most studies have looked at alphabetic languages like English and Italian.

   g. However, Chinese relies more heavily on symbols called orthographs in written communication.

   h. Tests using a magnetic resonance imaging machine were conducted on Chinese children with dyslexia to determine how their brains reacted when they tried to read.

Name _____ Course _____ Date _____

i. A completely different region of the brain was activated in the impaired Chinese readers than in their English counterparts.

j. The study highlights the importance of paying attention to differences in languages when trying to treat this very complicated disorder.

Name _____ Course _____ Date _____

B2. IDENTIFYING PHRASES. If you have problems completing this exercise, refer to pages 60-63 of *A Canadian Writer's Guide*. Answers appear at the end of this workbook.

1. **Underline and identify the type of phrase used in each of the following sentences: 1 = prepositional phrase, 2 = participial phrase, 3 = gerund phrase, 4 = infinitive phrase, 5 = appositive phrase, 6 = absolute phrase.**

    a. The current premier of Alberta, Ralph Klein, has said that this will be his last term in office.

    b. Smoking cigarettes was her downfall.

    c. Elvis loved to live dangerously.

    d. Given the enormous cost of living in the city, Doug has managed very well.

    e. Revenge is a dish best eaten cold.

    f. In the coffee pot, there was still enough for an extra cup.

    g. The cat loves sitting in my lap.

    h. My sisters, Diane and Lena, really enjoy dancing at nightclubs.

    i. Tears streaming down her face, Brenda watched Nate leave.

    j. Ruthie and Nikolai frequently get into arguments, mainly over money.

2. **Underline and identify the type of phrase used in each of the following sentences: 1 = prepositional phrase, 2 = participial phrase, 3 = gerund phrase, 4 = infinitive phrase, 5 = appositive phrase, 6 = absolute phrase.**

    a. Living well is the best revenge.

    b. Asleep at the wheel, he drove off the road.

    c. One eye open, my cat peered at me from across the pillow.

    d. Tired after a hard day's work, Gwynneth couldn't wait to get into the tub.

    e. The entrepreneur's cars, a sports car and a BMW, were parked in the driveway.

    f. To be honest, I will never in a million years give my consent.

    g. To have been part of the Olympics was the greatest honour for the gymnast.

    h. Most people enjoy having a manicure.

    i. Winning the lottery was the furthest thing from my mind.

    j. Fred and Ginger liked to dance the night away.

Name _____ Course _____ Date _____

3. **Identify the type of phrase used in each of the sentences:**
   1 = prepositional phrase 2 = participial phrase, 3 = gerund phrase, 4 = infinitive phrase, 5 = appositive phrase, 6 = absolute phrase.

   The International Friends of Literature is an organization dedicated to the creation of peace through culture and literature. It was founded in 1985 in Haifa, Israel and registered as a voluntary association in 1987. This organization strives to illustrate how important it is to analyze fictional tales of war and violence when researching peace. Studying literature is an important part of peace research because it enables individuals to examine the different values of peace studies in a variety of situations, thus helping to reinforce many of the key concepts of peace. In fiction, the values of peace and the destructiveness of war are presented in a way that allows researchers to explore alternative methods to achieve conflict resolution without endorsing or rejecting methods uncritically. As a result, literature may have a decisive role in shaping peace processes.

Name _____ Course _____ Date _____

B2. Constructing Clauses. If you have problems completing this exercise, refer to pages 60-63 of *A Canadian Writer's Guide*. Suggested answers appear at the end of this workbook.

1. **For each of the following sentences, create the type of phrase named.**

    a. [prepositional phrase] _____, Denise decided to quit her job as the assistant manager.

    b. The iPod, [appositive phrase] _____, has become one of the most popular electronic gadgets in recent years.

    c. [gerund phrase] _____ is difficult when you do not have the right tools.

    d. [infinitive phrase] _____ is the greatest challenge that students face today once they graduate.

    e. [prepositional phrase] _____, electricity use usually rises because people turn on their air conditioners.

    f. Mrs. Lupinski, [appositive phrase] _____, showed up to the wedding in a formal gown and crutches.

    g. [absolute phrase] _____, Tito collapsed on the couch and slept until noon the next day.

    h. Karim disliked [gerund phrase] _____ when he moved from his home in Kenya.

    i. Working part-time [infinitive phrase] _____ is a reality that more Canadian students are facing.

    j. When he saw his friends receiving awards for their artistic accomplishments, Jeremy began [prepositional phrase] _____ that he didn't take more risks in his life.

Name _____ Course _____ Date _____

B2. IDENTIFYING CLAUSES. If you have problems completing this exercise, refer to pages 60-63 of *A Canadian Writer's Guide*. Answers appear at the end of this workbook.

1. Underline, and using numbers, identify the dependent and independent clauses in the following paragraphs: 1 = independent clause, 2 = dependent clause.

North Americans are fat and getting fatter. Two out of three Americans are overweight or obese, and recent Canadian studies show the same trends developing here. When two teenage girls in the United States sued McDonald's for making them obese, documentary filmmaker Morgan Spurlock set out to discover what has made people so fat. The result is his film *Super Size Me*, a hilarious and often shocking look at the effects of fast food on the human body.

Spurlock conducted an experiment. He would subject himself to a diet of nothing but McDonald's fast food for 30 days. He allowed himself to eat only what was available over the counter at the restaurant. He had to eat every item on the McDonald's menu at least once, and he had to eat breakfast, lunch, and dinner every day. Throughout his experiment, he visited doctors and health professionals to track his decline in health. At the beginning of the film, Spurlock measured 6' 2" tall and weighed 185 pounds. His cholesterol was a healthy 168, his blood pressure 120/80, and his body fat measured 11%. A month later, Spurlock's weight had shot up to 210 pounds, his cholesterol was 230, and body fat had increased to 18%.

Super Size Me uses humour to present a harsh condemnation of the practices used to lure people, especially children, into eating fast food. McDonald's sets itself up for exactly the kind of lawsuit it was subjected to simply because of its targeting of children with clowns, "happy meals," and cartoons. The film ends, however, by reporting that the two teenage girls failed in their lawsuit against McDonald's and, shortly after, the United States Congress passed a law prohibiting people from suing fast food restaurants for obesity.

Name _____ Course _____ Date _____

2. Underline, and using numbers, identify the dependent and independent clauses in the following paragraphs: 1 = independent clause, 2 = dependent clause.

Almost half of Ontario's adults are overweight,(1) and measures need to be taken to reduce(1) what has become an obesity "epidemic".(2) These are the words of the province's chief medical officer said her annual report.(1) Dr. Sheila Basrur said(1) she was alarmed to find(2) that almost one out of every two adults in Ontario is overweight or obese.(2) The report also warns(1) that obesity among children aged seven to 13 tripled between 1981 and 1996.(2) In addition to contributing to heart disease, strokes, hypertentions and some forms of cancer, unhealthy weights are responsible for a dramatic rise in adult-onset diabetes.(1) When combined with sensible eating habits,(2) active living would improve the quality of life for everyone in the province.(1)

The report contains several recommendations for the Ontario government,(1) including a mass-media campaign to increase awareness of the benefits of maintaining a healthy weight. Basrur also asked the government to control food advertising aimed at children,(1) similar to measures in Quebec prohibiting advertising of some products to children under the age of 13.(2) The report also suggests(1) that the federal government act to phase out trans fat from processed foods and require large chain restaurants to disclose basic nutrition facts about the foods(2) they serve.(2) The report recommends(1) that the food industry decrease serving sizes, especially of snack foods and increase the use of user-friendly food labelling on large chain restaurant menus and take-out foods.(2) By taking steps to solve the problem of obesity now,(2) we will hopefully be reducing the burden on the healthcare system in the future.(1)

Name _____ Course _____ Date _____

SENTENCE ELEMENTS

S1. IDENTIFYING PARTS OF SENTENCES. If you have problems completing this exercise, refer to pages 71-74 in *A Canadian Writer's Guide*. Answers appear at the end of this workbook.

1. **Underline the complete subject in the following sentences, and write SS above the simple subject. If the subject is an understood *you*, insert it in parentheses.**

    a. Ads are the cave art of the twentieth century. —*Marshall McLuhan.*

    b. The ideal companion in bed is a good book. —*Robertson Davies*

    c. There is no blood in our history. —*Pierre Berton*

    d. To write simply is as difficult as to be good. —*Somerset Maugham*

    e. Writing is turning one's worst moments into money. —*J.P. Donleavy*

    f. Writers, like teeth, are divided into incisors and grinders. —*Walter Bagehot*

    g. To reveal art and conceal the artist is art's aim. —*Oscar Wilde*

    h. A great many people now reading and writing would be better employed keeping rabbits. —*Edith Sitwell*

    i. There are books of which the backs and covers are by far the best part. —*Charles Dickens*

    j. The devil doesn't make personal appearances. —*Morris Panych*

Name _____ Course _____ Date _____

2. Underline the complete subject in the following sentences, and write SS above the simple subject. If the subject is an understood *you*, insert it in parentheses.

   a. Every vital *development* in language is a development of feeling as well. —*T. S. Eliot*

   b. My *pencils* outlast their erasers. —*Vladimir Nabokov*

   c. *Words* pick up flavours and odours like butter in a refrigerator. —*John Steinbeck*

   d. Why shouldn't *we* quarrel about a word? —*G. K. Chesterton*

   e. The *art* of writing has for backbone some fierce attachment to an idea. —*Virginia Woolf*

   f. All good *writing* is swimming under water and holding your breath. —*F. Scott Fitzgerald*

   g. (*you*) Better far write twaddle or anything, anything, than nothing at all. —*Katherine Mansfield*

   h. *Language* is the archives of history. —*Ralph Waldo Emerson*

   i. A *poet* can survive everything but a misprint. —*Oscar Wilde*

   j. *I* believe in miracles in every area except writing. —*Isaac Bashevis Singer*

3. **Identify the direct objects (DO), indirect objects (IO), and object complements (OC) in the following sentences. If an object or complement is more than one word, bracket all of it when you identify it.**

   a. If you can't do the time, don't do the crime. —*Earl Work*
   b. Give a man an inch, and he thinks he's a ruler. —*Don Harron*
   c. Every writer is a frustrated actor who recites his lines in the hidden auditorium of his skull. —*Rod Serling*
   d. I wrote my first novel because I wanted to read it. —*Toni Morrison*
   e. He is the best orator who can turn men's ears into eyes – *Arabic proverb*
   f. Writing fiction has become a priestly business in countries that have lost their faith. —*Gore Vidal*
   g. When you catch an adjective, kill it. —*Mark Twain*
   h. Quotation confesses inferiority. —*Ralph Waldo Emerson*
   i. Real art has the capacity to make us nervous. —*Susan Sontag*
   j. A little inaccuracy sometimes saves tons of explanations. —*Saki*

Name _____ Course _____ Date _____

4. Identify the direct objects (DO), indirect objects (IO), and object complements (OC) in the following sentences. If an object or complement is more than one word, bracket all of it when you identify it.

  a. No word was ever as effective as a rightly timed pause. —*Mark Twain*

  b. No human being can really understand another, and no one can arrange another's happiness. —*Graham Greene*

  c. Art attempts to find in the universe, in matter as well as in the facts of life, what is fundamental, enduring, essential. —*Saul Bellow*

  d. I'll make him an offer he can't refuse. —*Mario Puzo*

  e. Parents are the bones on which children sharpen their teeth. —*Peter Ustinov*

  f. The true writer has nothing to say. —*Alain Robbe-Grillet*

  g. If a man hasn't discovered something that he will die for, he isn't fit to live. —*Martin Luther King*

  h. Don't count your chickens before they hatch. – *English proverb*

  i. The prayer of the chicken hawk does not get him the chicken. —*Swahili proverb*

  j. The eggs do not teach the hen. —*Russian proverb*

Name _____ Course _____ Date _____

S2. IDENTIFYING SENTENCE PATTERNS. If you have problems completing this exercise, refer to pages 74-76 in *A Canadian Writer's Guide.* Answers appear at the end of this workbook.

1. For each of the following ten sentences, identify the sentence pattern—e.g., Pattern 1 (subject-verb), Pattern 2 (subject-verb-subject complement), Pattern 3 (subject-verb-direct object), Pattern 4 (subject-verb-indirect object-direct object), Pattern 5 (subject-verb-direct object-object complement).

   a. _____ David and Maureen wrote their certification exams this morning.

   b. _____ Dr. Davis regards homeopathic medicine a hoax.

   c. _____ Garth seemed preoccupied today in class.

   d. _____ She gave her passport to the clerk in the hotel.

   e. _____ My professor wears the same jacket each Monday.

   f. _____ The chain reaction is the basis of nuclear power.

   g. _____ Mandy practices her violin daily.

   h. _____ Doctors feel the discovery to be a breakthrough in treating depression.

   i. _____ The firm is building children a new playground in the park.

   j. _____ Prolonged exposure to the chemical can be fatal.

2. For each of the following ten sentences, identify the sentence pattern—e.g., Pattern 1 (subject-verb), Pattern 2 (subject-verb-subject complement), Pattern 3 (subject-verb-direct object), Pattern 4 (subject-verb-indirect object-direct object), Pattern 5 (subject-verb-direct object-object complement).

   a. _____ The debating club elected Michael president.

   b. _____ The lab assistants ate five pizzas at their office Christmas party.

   c. _____ The telephone rings constantly.

   d. _____ The guidance counsellor gave me the best advice.

   e. _____ Some people consider musicals dull.

   f. _____ Lear will never forgive his daughters.

   g. _____ Hamlet hesitates too much.

   h. _____ Lady Macbeth gives her husband the motivation to murder the king.

   i. _____ *Titus Andronicus* shocks theatre audiences.

   j. _____ Shakespeare uses violence in many of his plays.

Name _____ Course _____ Date _____

S3. IDENTIFYING SENTENCE TYPES. If you have problems completing this exercise, refer to pages 76-77 in *A Canadian Writer's Guide*. Answers appear at the end of this workbook.

1. Identify the following sentences as simple, compound, complex, or compound-complex.

a. We hope you prosper.
   _____

b. I wish you luck.
   _____

c. In order to thrive in business today, you need to diversify.
   _____

d. Cutting down the chestnut tree, Rohan discovered the real size of his front yard.
   _____

e. Doris's mother kissed her, her father shook her hand, and her brother snapped her picture after the ceremony.
   _____

f. The desire to write grows with writing.
   _____

g. You may write at any time if you are determined enough.
   _____

h. Idan admitted during the meeting that he hadn't met his quarterly targets.
   _____

i. Mr. Daniels, whose son was in the audience, stuttered, stammered and finally fainted on stage.
   _____

j. Marvous realized the extent of her mistake, and, after stopping to think for a minute, she did not know how to correct it.
   _____

Name _____ Course _____ Date _____

2. Identify the following sentences as simple, compound, complex, or compound-complex.

a. Never in my whole life have I seen such a mess.
_____

b. Sheldon quit his job; he never worked in a packing plant again.
_____

c. You are entitled to your own opinion; however, you should keep it to yourself.
_____

d. I know exactly what you are thinking.
_____

e. The upper two chambers of the heart, which are called atria, are thin-walled reservoirs; they readily distend to collect blood that pours in from the veins between beats.
_____

f. I saw what you did, and I know who you are.
_____

g. There are basically two types of stethoscopes.
_____

h. Smile when you say that.
_____

i. A fool and his money are soon parted.
_____

j. If you don't eat your vegetables, you'll be sorry.
_____

Name _____ Course _____ Date _____

S5. EDITING SENTENCES FOR VARIETY. If you have problems completing this exercise, refer to pages 80-82 in *A Canadian Writer's Guide*. Suggested answers appear at the end of this workbook.

1. Edit the following paragraph to improve its use of sentence variety.

Going back to school in September can be traumatic. For a student, it can be expensive. September can also be frustrating because the weather is still usually so beautiful. For a student, September means a lot of anxiety because of new responsibilities. Trying to get used to a new schedule can be difficult. This is true particularly if you have spent the summer sleeping in and taking advantage of the time off. Getting used to a new place of residence is also often challenging. Leaving the comfort and security of your parents' home can be a trial. School offers rewards to a student. Students get opportunities to meet new people. Students also get a chance to learn something new. Along with these new chances come many fears and pressures. Students need to appreciate the novelty of their lives. They can then try to forget about the anxieties they feel. September doesn't have to be a problem. Students who are organized will prosper. Students who are prepared to face change in their lives will find excitement and happiness.

Name _____ Course _____ Date _____

2. Edit the following paragraph to improve its use of sentence variety.

This is the age of neuroscience. The human brain is a maze of wisdom. We are finally exploring the home frontier in earnest. Much of this new data is due to the incredible tools we now have to investigate the human brain. CT scans and MRI machines make it possible for researchers to view changes in brain chemistry. The brain is in action during these studies. There are so many new findings coming out every day. Some are straightforward. Others are controversial and even puzzling. For example, about a quarter of the brain is involved in visual processing. This is more than for all other senses. Scientists now believe that there is not a single memory centre. A memory is most likely stored in the same areas of the brain that were involved in the perception, processing and analysis of the original input. Remembering is the re-experiencing of the original event. It is probably a reactivation of the same neuronal circuit. Finally, long thought impossible, human neurogenesis has now been confirmed in some brain regions. This is the process of growing new brain cells. We still do not know for certain what these new brain cells are for.

Name _____ Course _____ Date _____

GRAMMATICAL SENTENCES

G1. SENTENCE FRAGMENTS. If you have problems completing this exercise, refer to pages 89-91 of *A Canadian Writer's Guide*. Answers appear at the end of this workbook.

1. **Correct any sentence fragments in the sentences below by rewriting them as complete sentences or by connecting them to another sentence. Some sentences may be correct as they stand.**

    Example:

    > To be all I can be. That is my personal goal in life.
    >
    > <u>**My personal goal in life is to be all I can be.**</u>

    a. Many students working in Professor James's laboratory last summer.
    _____

    b. Do you think you are going to quit school? Over my dead body.
    _____

    c. Ella liked living on the edge of the escarpment. Which is why she dreaded having to leave her current job.
    _____

    d. Ilya found himself spending a lot of time in the penalty box. Enforcer being his role on the team.
    _____

    e. David chose a cake for the party. The chocolate one that appealed to him the most.
    _____

    f. She was resigned to her fate. Having surrendered herself to the authorities.
    _____

18 G1 *Sentence Fragments*

Name _____ Course _____ Date _____

g. There were door prizes at the year-end party given by the organizers. To entice people to show up.

_____

h. The programs runs all year round. With only a short break between each semester.

_____

i. You will soon be evicted. Which is just fine by me.

_____

j. He stared at her in awe. Never in a million years believing her story.

_____

Name _____ Course _____ Date _____

2. **Correct any sentence fragments in the sentences below by rewriting them as complete sentences or by connecting them to another sentence. Some sentences may be correct as they stand. See the example in the exercise above.**

   a. Never in a million years. That's how often I intend to contact my former employer.

   _____

   b. Malcolm lay on the couch for the rest of the night. Digesting his dinner.

   _____

   c. Email is a great waste of time. Which many companies are finding out.

   _____

   d. Surely you are not going to quit your job. Not in this lifetime

   _____

   e. Experience is what you get when you don't get what you want.

   _____

   f. Working overtime is not always profitable. Because the taxes go up as well.

   _____

   g. Sleeping through the service. Each of the Simpsons had a dream.

   _____

   h. Do not deny your love for Sigismund. Not here, not now.

   _____

   i. Solving exercises is easier. Whereas editing can be challenging.

   _____

   j. Although Laura has had a lot of experience as a dog trainer.

   _____

20   G1 *Sentence Fragments*

Name _____ Course _____ Date _____

G1. RUN-ON SENTENCES. If you have any problems completing this exercise, refer to pages 92-93 of *A Canadian Writer's Guide*. Answers appear at the end of this workbook.

1. Correct any fused sentences or comma splices you find in the following sentences. Some sentences may be correct as they stand.

Example:

> Buy now, pay later.
>
> <u>Buy now. Pay later.</u>

a. I may procrastinate I don't quit though.

b. The neighbour's dog overturned our garbage can, then he scattered litter everywhere.

c. Read the fine print on any contract before you sign, it could save you headaches later on.

d. To be or not to be, that is the question.

e. Some people work to live, others live to work.

f. I love you, you're perfect, now change.

g. People can live for two months without food; they would die in a week without water.

h. I know the answer, what was the question again?

i. She's so stubborn you can't argue with her.

j. Smile sweetly, but be sincere.

G2 Run-on Sentences   21

Name _____ Course _____ Date _____

2. Correct any fused sentences or comma splices you find in the following sentences. Some sentences may be correct as they stand. See the example in the exercise above.

a. There was no hockey on TV this year, most people found something else to do.
_____

b. Life is a beach I guess death is the deep end.
_____

c. Reality shows are inexpensive to produce, this is why there are so many on TV.
_____

d. Few realize that these shows are often as scripted and staged as sitcoms or soap operas nevertheless people will watch them eagerly.
_____

e. Dog shows fascinate me, it doesn't matter which breed is best in show.
_____

f. You cannot base your life on what you see on TV shows if you do you're headed for some bad news.
_____

g. Situation comedies are often about people over forty who are single and dating, usually these shows don't bear much resemblance to life.
_____

h. It's ragweed season, all my friends with allergies are sneezing.
_____

i. Gym glass was his nemesis, he lacked coordination and was always picked last for team sports.
_____

j. Cell phones are dangerous on the road hence drivers should use them only when parked.
_____

Name _____ Course _____ Date _____

G2. SUBJECT-VERB AGREEMENT. If you have problems completing this exercise, refer to pages 93-94 of *A Canadian Writer's Guide*. Answers appear at the end of this workbook.

1. Correct any errors in subject and verb agreement you find in the following sentences. Some sentences may be correct as they stand.

Example:

Neither Britney Spears nor Ashley Simpson have any talent.

Neither Britney Spears nor Ashley Simpson has any talent.

a. There is two bottles of beer left in the cooler.

b. A number of us is going to the carnival.

c. Economics is my worst subject.

d. Edmund's favourite snack are pretzels and beer.

e. Love and patience is required in the daycare centre.

f. Neither he nor his friends has ever appeared on television.

g. Each of the dogs wear a tag.

h. There is two cars parked in the driveway.

i. Neither Reneé nor the Johnsons has to wait for their awards now.

j. One of the people given the task has been reassigned elsewhere in the company.

G3 *Subject-Verb Agreement* 23

Name _____ Course _____ Date _____

2. **Correct any errors in subject and verb agreement you find in the following sentences. Some sentences may be correct as they stand. See the example in the exercise above.**

   a. Bits of angel food cake was always to be found on the kitchen floor.

   b. Items available for sale on ebay.ca is plentiful but sometimes of questionable quality.

   c. The presence of critics in the audience have always disturbed me during performances.

   d. Nearly everyone on the board approve of the latest pay increases.

   e. Neither management nor the players appears to be ready to make any concessions

   f. At CBC the history of film and television in Canada come alive.

   g. Judie was the only one of my friends who insist that I should try harder.

   h. The key concern of the committee members are the perks and the use of the free limousine.

   i. Every year a number of fish with high level of Mercury is caught in that river.

   j. Owning a house and a car have placed considerable stress on their marriage.

24 G3 *Subject-Verb Agreement*

Name _____ Course _____ Date _____

G2. VERB TENSE AND MOOD AGREEMENT. If you have problems completing this exercise, refer to pages 98-99 of *A Canadian Writer's Guide.* Answers appear at the end of this workbook.

1. Correct errors in verb tense in the following sentences. Some sentences may be correct as they stand.

Example:

> I asked her to go to the party, and she says yes.
> **I asked her to go to the party, and she said yes.**

a. One person hands out the brochure, and the other will ask passersby if they would like more information about the service.

b. The candidate for the position is very forthcoming. Too much information about why she was fired from her previous job was given to the interviewers.

c. As I was finishing the report, you could hear the committee members getting restless in the audience.

d. Thanksgiving dinner at my parents' house usually ends the same way every year. We snacked, ate dinner, and fell asleep on the couch.

e. The last Usher concert was really great. I go with my friend, and we stand two feet away from the stage the whole time.

Name _____ Course _____ Date _____

f. In *Fifth Business*, Robertson Davies created the town of Deptford from his memories of small-town Ontario. Similarly, Alice Munro creates Hanratty as a substitute for her hometown, Hanover, Ontario.

_____
_____
_____

g. Boxing day sales usually offer consumers a chance to save money, but they also gave merchants an opportunity to clear out old merchandise.

_____
_____

h. After the fire, the rescuers bandaged the cat and prepared to take it to a shelter. It meows pitifully.

_____

i. We walked through the Toronto's deserted streets at night until, finally, we find the Hockey Hall of Fame.

_____
_____

j. I open my lunch box. And there it was: another corned beef sandwich.

_____

Name _____ Course _____ Date _____

2. Correct errors in verb tense in the following sentences. Some sentences may be correct as they stand. See the example in the exercise above.

a. The comedian tells a joke, and the audience laughed hysterically.

b. The teacher held a pop quiz. You could have heard a pin drop.

c. The actress opened the envelope. The winner is Sean Penn.

d. After years of struggling to become popular, Shania Twain moves to Switzerland where she is unknown.

e. She asked what my name was, and I say John.

f. I have lived in this town since I am ten years old.

g. The power went off because the storm is so fierce.

h. You would be shocked by what we saw yesterday.

i. After scoring well on the first test, Michelle is convinced that she will pass the course with ease.

j. In the novel *The Life of Pi,* Yann Martel retold the story of Noah's Ark.

Name _____ Course _____ Date _____

G2. PRONOUN-ANTECEDENT AGREEMENT. If you have problems completing this exercise, refer to pages 99-100 of *A Canadian Writer's Guide*. Answers appear at the end of this workbook.

1. Correct any errors in pronoun-antecedent agreement in the following sentences. Some sentences may be correct as they stand.

Example:

Everyone who is going home has their reasons.

<u>Everyone who is going home has his reasons. (*or* her reasons)</u>

a. No one knew what they might be expected to do.

b. The audience clapped their hands and registered its approval.

c. Each of the administrative assistants wants a printer and scanner.

d. Every company has their own way of interviewing new applicants.

e. An employee should keep their personal email separate from their work messages.

f. Anyone who wears a thong should have their head examined.

g. If a person chooses to room alone on the trip, they will still have to pay double occupancy.

h. The board voted to give itself a raise after they dealt with the grievances presented to them.

i. Every participant should select their songs prior to the competition deadline.

j. My family has eccentric taste, but they sure know how to put on a show.

Name _____ Course _____ Date _____

2. Correct any errors in pronoun-antecedent agreement in the following sentences. Some sentences may be correct as they stand. See the example in the exercise above.

a. One of the students must give their oral presentations tomorrow in class.

b. Why is the sea bass an endangered species? They are being overfished in certain parts of the world because they are considered a delicacy.

c. No one should have to give up their dreams.

d. If anyone knows of the suspect's whereabouts, they should contact the police immediately.

e. Everybody prays that it's their lottery numbers that get picked every Friday night.

f. Each of the women hoped that the courses they were taking would lead to employment.

g. If anybody doesn't like the music I'm playing, they can go somewhere else.

h. I lent someone the videotapes, and they passed them on to their friends.

i. Each member of the committee must submit their candidate for consideration by the end of the week.

j. If a driver leaves the scene of an accident, they will lose their licence.

G5 Pronoun-Antecedent Agreement **29**

Name _____ Course _____ Date _____

G3. UNCLEAR PRONOUN REFERENCE. If you have any problems completing this exercise, refer to pages 101-102 of *A Canadian Writer's Guide*. Answers appear at the end of this workbook.

1. Correct any errors in pronoun reference in the following sentences. Some sentences may be correct as they stand.

Example:

> When the dog sat on the chair, it groaned.
>
> <u>The chair groaned when the dog sat on it.</u>

a. Sean told Liam stay away from his little brother.

b. Denise quit school, which explains why she is waiting on tables.

c. Drunk drivers cause accidents. This should not happen.

d. In Georgian Bay, they have a three-month long tourist season.

e. Their favourite beer in Australia is Victoria Bitter.

f. It is bad luck for you to walk under a ladder.

g. The lamb followed Mary to school, which was against the rule.

h. She couldn't say goodbye to her aunt because she was sick.

i. When very little rain falls, it greatly affects the growth of the crops in the spring.

j. When Tamecka asked Ms. Fracus for a raise, she didn't know what to say.

Name _____ Course _____ Date _____

2. Correct any errors in pronoun reference in the following sentences. Some sentences may be correct as they stand. See the example in the exercise above.

a. The runner that made the team at the last minute ended up placing first at the meet.
_____

b. Many people believe that interviewing processes are unreliable unless you carry out a strict hiring policy.
_____

c. We thought that seats would be available at the last moment. Since the star of the show is so popular, this turned out to be unrealistic.
_____

d. I'd like to become an electrician because it pays well.
_____

e. Since the tutorial leader could write so well, it gave us the opportunity to practice our skills.
_____

f. When Phillip put the car in the garage, it had a bent fender.
_____

g. In Brazil they speak Portuguese, not Spanish.
_____

h. Be sure to visit Harbourfront's skating rink where they offer lessons every weekday.
_____

i. If you are hungry, you can visit the snack bar, where they are available fresh and at a discount.
_____

j. Chantelle decided not to marry the man that she'd been dating for the past six years.
_____

G6 *Unclear Pronoun Reference*

Name _____ Course _____ Date _____

G3. MISPLACED MODIFIERS. If you have any problems completing this exercise, refer to page 103-104 of *A Canadian Writer's Guide*. Answers appear at the end of this workbook

1. Correct any errors in the use of modifiers in the following sentences. Some sentences may be correct as they stand.

Example:

      I only ate one pizza.

    <u>I ate only one pizza.</u>

a. Scratching each other's backs, the tourists observed the gorillas.

b. He keeps an ashtray on his desk, which he seldom uses.

c. Being an only child, I was almost free to do anything I desired.

d. Enclosed by barbed wire in their natural habitat, the children watched the crocodiles.

e. The pills came from this bottle he swallowed.

f. The supervisor was informed that the work was completed last week.

g. Rhonda's hobby was building furniture, which she found relaxing.

h. This morning the press reported that the building would be torn down.

i. No one hardly knew the answer.

j. I only ate and drank enough to keep from being hungry.

Name _____ Course _____ Date _____

2. Correct any errors in the use of modifiers in the following sentences. Some sentences may be correct as they stand.

a. Wearing a pink skirt, George took his sister to see the exhibition.

b. Kim received a letter about a show on portrait making from an old friend.

c. Hopefully, it won't rain on the weekend.

d. The nurse admitted that she didn't know CPR as well as she should have after her supervisor questioned her for over an hour.

e. We saw a skunk driving home late last night.

f. The prime minister was accused of mishandling the campaign funds by the media.

g. The old pictures showed a woman in bed eating an ice cream cone.

h. You will just need to plant one package of seeds.

i. Answering questions can be nerve-racking in front of a jury.

j. The assailant was described as a tall man with a black moustache weighing approximately 150 pounds.

G7 Misplaced Modifiers 33

Name _____ Course _____ Date _____

G3. DANGLING MODIFIERS. If you have any problems completing this exercise, refer to pages 104-105 of *A Canadian Writer's Guide*. Answers appear at the end of this workbook.

1. Correct any errors in the use of modifiers in the following sentences. Some sentences may be correct as they stand.

Example:

Sleeping in every morning, lots of classes were missed.

<u>**Sleeping in every morning, Gunther missed lots of classes.**</u>

a. When using a drill, caution is required.

b. To succeed in school, a great deal of reading is necessary.

c. A comedian at heart, her students often laughed during her class.

d. After studying all the examples, the math questions suddenly became easier.

e. When you are connecting the battery cables, the engine should not be running.

f. By raising the interest rates, the market was adversely affected.

g. As a new employee, the probationary period seemed threatening.

h. Dieting rigorously for over six months, Mrs. Jones's husband thought his wife looked divinely slim.

i. After criticizing my efforts, I was fired.

j. She found the body working on the night shift.

34 G8 *Dangling Modifiers*

Name _____ Course _____ Date _____

2. Correct any errors in the use of modifiers in the following sentences. Some sentences may be correct as they stand. See the example in the exercise above.

a. Answering the phone, a shudder went through the babysitter.

b. After leaving the ship, the strange birds were the first things we noticed.

c. Yesterday while visiting friends, the hostess served us French ice cream.

d. While starting the car this morning, the sun shone through the windshield.

e. When working overtime at the convenience store, it was hard for me to forget how often such stores had been held up in the past.

f. Although overwhelmed with credit card debt, the leather chair was still irresistible to Michael.

g. While looking for my purse, a security guard asked if he could be of service.

h. Changing the oil every 6 000 kilometres, the car seemed to run much better.

i. Raised in Nova Scotia, it is natural to miss the smell of the sea.

j. Sitting on the balcony, the sound of the surf reached the ears of the happy tourists.

G8 Dangling Modifiers **35**

Name _____ Course _____ Date _____

G3. FAULTY PARALLEL STRUCTURE. If you have any problems completing this exercise, refer to page 105 of *A Canadian Writer's Guide*. Answers appear at the end of this workbook.

1. Correct any errors in the use of parallel structure in the following sentences. Some sentences may be correct as they stand.

Example:

Eating chocolate is expensive, bad for your teeth, and it makes you gain weight.
<u>Eating chocolate is expensive, bad for your teeth, and fattening.</u>

a. You either vacate the premises, or I call the police.

b. Having practiced, prayed and hard training, the Richview Scots football team placed first in the provincial competition.

c. Having done all the chapter exercises, studied the review sheets, and all the formulas were memorized, Henry knew he'd pass the final exam.

d. People who believe in astrology are frequently dismissed as gullible, superstitious, and they liked to have their egos stroked.

e. Dr. Shulman attributes his financial success to careful planning, keeping up with current events, and a wealthy wife.

f. Mahatma Ghandi was the inspiration of many 20th century leaders because of his ability to perceive the root of a problem, encouragement of others to support him, and finding non-violent methods of change.

Name _____ Course _____ Date _____

g. The assistant's work included writing, teaching, and to edit his papers carefully because his supervisor saw them.

_____
_____

h. Martha has studied floristry, needlework, and how to decorate.

_____

i. We regret not being able to ship the order at once and that we must ask you to be patient.

_____

j. In both the West and in eastern countries, there are concerns about economic development.

_____

G9 *Faulty Parallel Structure*

Name _____ Course _____ Date _____

2. Correct any errors in the use of parallel structure in the following sentences. Some sentences may be correct as they stand. See the example in the exercise above.

a. Ethel finds it harder to be critical of others than being critical of herself.

b. My work involves teaching, marking papers, and I constantly look for a better job.

c. Being a foreigner, not speaking the language, and all alone, Freda decided to join a guided tour of Banff.

d. The mentor's job is to help you fix your papers, write more skilfully, and to understand your assignments better.

e. At the pottery exhibit, we saw potters make ashtrays, dishes, bowls, vases, and paint finished items.

f. The summer we went to England, we saw many plays, ate out a lot, and we took a boat down the Thames.

g. How much quieter it is to live in Dundas than the downtown core of the city.

h. The family decided to rent a cottage in the Lakes Region for a month and that Bianca and I could use it for a month.

i. Driver education teaches students to become better drivers by obeying traffic laws, never to exceed speed limits, and always to watch the road signs.

j. Geoff liked camping, biking, and building canoes.

Name _____ Course _____ Date _____

USAGE AND DICTION

U1. REDUNDANCY AND WORDINESS. If you have problems completing this exercise, refer to page 147 of *A Canadian Writer's Guide.* Answers appear at the end of this workbook.

1. Edit the following sentences, being careful to tend to redundant expressions.

a. This printer operates at the rate of four pages per minute.

b. The desire to express oneself is a universal craving that is common to all people.

c. In today's society, the widespread use of narcotics among the people has created other problems such as crime and the spread of diseases.

d. The international airport that serves the city of Toronto is located in close proximity to the city itself.

e. At this point in time, we would like to tell you that your van has been repaired and can be picked up at your earliest convenience.

f. For the downtown installation, the project manager tentatively planned to operate with a round-the-clock schedule.

g. In my opinion, I think that the cheque should be returned to the customer.

U1 *Usage and Diction* **39**

Name _____ Course _____ Date _____

    h. We attach our statement in the amount of $500 in respect of services rendered during the period of May through August.

    _____

    _____

    i. If you plan on repairing your SUV, you would be well advised to secure a cost estimate in advance of proceeding.

    _____

    _____

    j. It was decided by the senate that its members were in agreement with my boss's proposal to terminate my position for an indefinite period of time.

    _____

    _____

Name _____ Course _____ Date _____

2. Edit the following sentences, being careful to tend to redundant expressions.

a. Your job will be the preparation of every single piece of information that is to be received by each and every employee within the entire precinct.

_____
_____

b. What I really would like to say is that I intend to quit at the earliest possible opportunity.

_____

c. Her new outfit consisted of a dress that was red in colour, which she decided to wear with a sweater that was woven from lambswool.

_____
_____

d. In my personal opinion, it is a significant fact that jobs have become more and more difficult for students who are just graduating to find.

_____
_____

e. Because of the fact that she is older than I am, my parents had a tendency to trust her judgement more than mine.

_____
_____

f. Your charge card is enclosed; you will find it a great convenience if you will use it while you are shopping at any one of our stores.

_____
_____

U1 *Usage and Diction*

g. The end of the corridor terminates at a small door that is green in colour.

h. The first time Sheila failed her driver's test, she realized her speed must be more slower if she were to be successful the next time around.

i. At the present time, the main concern of the board is whether the president has the ability to continue.

j. On the third day of the month of September, the Premier officially opened the east wing of the Hospital for Sick Children.

Name _____ Course _____ Date _____

U1. APPROPRIATE CONNOTATIONS AND SLANG. If you have problems completing this exercise, refer to page 148 of *A Canadian Writer's Guide.* Answers appear at the end of this workbook.

1. Edit these sentences, removing language that is inappropriate to an academic context.

   a. Seventy-five percent of North American households have wheels of some kind.
   _____

   b. Irregardless of her political problems in the past, Kim Campbell now holds a prestigious position.
   _____

   c. You have to be aggressive when driving in the Montreal.
   _____

   d. The chauffeur was raked over the coals for his part in the fatal accident.
   _____

   e. Symptoms of influenza include sore throat, coughing, headache, and barfing.
   _____

   f. After being refused a reprieve, the prisoner chewed down his last meal and waited for the execution.
   _____

   g. The Leafs fans were totally bummed out when their team blew it in the playoffs again.
   _____

   h. Students are encouraged to touch base with their advisors at least weekly.
   _____

   i. Theckla wasn't happy when she found out she had totally bombed the physics final exam.
   _____

   j. Students who ace the examination will be assured of a good final grade.
   _____

Name _____ Course _____ Date _____

2. Edit these sentences, removing language that is inappropriate to an academic context.

a. Tuition is expensive, but it will not break the bank if students prepare for their education carefully.

_____

b. The powers that be have decreed that no one may drink in this province until the age of nineteen.

_____
_____

c. The marketing teacher dissed Oswald in front of the whole class for talking on his cell phone.

_____

d. Municipal governments have put the squeeze on property owners to collect more taxes.

_____

e. Garth and Tito bounced their English class and decided to play pool in the student lounge instead.

_____

f. Drivers who knock back a few too many could face charges.

_____

g. Another 500 employees got the axe at Nortel Communications this week.

_____

h. Tupac Shakur bit the dust in a drive by in Vegas.

_____

i. Warren Buffet and Bill Gates have cleaned up in their respective professions and are among the richest people in the world.

_____
_____

j. The criminal shot off his mouth about his guilt in the robbery and got thrown in jail.

_____

Name _____ Course _____ Date _____

U1. CLICHÉS. If you have problems completing this exercise, refer to page 150 of *A Canadian Writer's Guide.* Suggested answers appear at the end of this workbook.

1. **Replace the clichés in the following sentences with fresh expressions.**

    a. The professor was a quick as a whip when answering questions on general relativity.

    b. Denise could be as stubborn as a mule when it came to choosing paint colours for the house.

    c. After hearing Stephen Lewis speak about the crisis in Africa, I decided to take him up on his suggestions.

    d. Herman's explanation of the theory of communicative action was as clear as mud.

    e. The director's misuse of the department's funds is a crying shame.

    f. After winning a second term in office, President Bush has found it easier to stick to his guns.

    g. Hume's *Treatise Concerning Human Understanding* is as dry as dust.

    h. I have to leave for school at the crack of dawn on Tuesdays and Thursdays.

    i. Opposing points of view to the new administration are few and far between.

    j. Read my lips: There will be no make up test for this chapter.

U1 *Clichés* **45**

Name _____ Course _____ Date _____

U1. IDIOMS. If you have problems completing this exercise, refer to pages 152-153 of *A Canadian Writer's Guide*. Answers appear at the end of this workbook.

1. In the following sentences replace errors in the use of idiomatic expressions. Some sentences may stand as they are.

a. The general public did not want to abide with the decision of the Supreme Court.

b. Be sure and answer all the questions completely before turning the page.

c. I intend on marrying Dexter as soon as the divorce is final.

d. Why do you think white-collar crime should be treated differently than fraud or embezzlement?

e. The look on her face showed that she was angry at her brother.

f. You have to try and think of a time when you were happier in your life.

g. Her sister was envious over her new dishwasher.

h. Lance could not gather the courage to ask her to a date.

i. What type of a person do you think I am?

j. Work is preferable than prison.

Name _____ Course _____ Date _____

U2. PRONOUN CASE. If you have problems completing this exercise, refer to pages 154-155 of *A Canadian Writer's Guide.* Answers appear at the end of this workbook.

1. **Correct problems with pronoun case in the following sentences. Some sentences may be correct as they stand.**

   a. Between you and I, I couldn't believe that the Americans had re-elected George W. Bush for President.
   b. The problem with your getting a pierced tongue is that it could become infected.
   c. The blame must be accepted by you and I.
   d. Border shopping used to be common among us Canadians.
   e. The amateur plays hockey better than him.
   f. What were you and her talking about?
   g. The supervisor asked Frances and I to work overtime.
   h. We are the only ones who should take the exam: my brother and me.
   i. The police officer gave the parking ticket to my husband and myself.
   j. Cathy and us ate all the cake at the birthday party.

2. **Correct problems with pronoun case in the following sentences. Some sentences may be correct as they stand.**

   a. The professor asked her and I to show our work to the rest of the class.
   b. Him and his dad run the whole business together.
   c. Me learning this information might make be a better writer one day.
   d. Between you and me, grammar can be tedious.
   e. When you saw Pat and me, we were late for an appointment.
   f. We instructors all agree that plagiarism is reprehensible.
   g. That was him on MuchMusic the other night.
   h. My wife weighs ten pounds more than me.
   i. They speak Spanish better than us.
   j. Only two people were interviewed: Larry and me.

Name _____ Course _____ Date _____

U3. PRONOUN CHOICE. If you have problems completing this exercise, refer to pages 157-158 of *A Canadian Writer's Guide*. Answers appear at the end of this workbook.

1. **Correct problems with who or whom in the following sentences. Some sentences may be correct as they stand.**

    a. The workers who were building the residence went on strike.

    b. Daniel could not remember who he'd given the papers to.

    c. We have met the lawyer who you were speaking of.

    d. There is no one in the room whom does not know the answer.

    e. Whom do you think will answer the summons?

    f. Whomever told you that was wrong.

    g. He is someone whom I believe always tells the truth.

    h. James, who I consider an ally, advised me to take this action.

    i. Whoever was knocking on the door is now ringing the doorbell.

    j. Whom do you think is likely to win the next *Canadian Idol* competition?

2. **Choose the appropriate pronoun, that or which, in the following sentences, and adjust the punctuation appropriately. Some sentences may be correct as they stand.**

    a. The group which I belong to is not political.

    b. That group, that I joined on the weekend, is dedicated to weight loss.

    c. The painting that you are referring to hangs in the Prada.

    d. That painting I gave you was priceless.

    e. The position that he played was quarterback.

    f. That yoga position, which I learned yesterday, is very difficult to sustain without practice.

    g. The DVD player which I bought only last year is already obsolete.

    h. Most DVD players that are available today can play MP3s, music files which are compressed to save space on a disc.

    i. The house which she owns is badly in need of repair.

    j. Cooking which is a useful skill should be taught in every high school.

48 U2 *Pronoun Choice*

Name _____ Course _____ Date _____

U4. AGREEMENT AND COLLECTIVE NOUNS. If you have problems completing this exercise, refer to page 158 of *A Canadian Writer's Guide*. Answers appear at the end of this workbook.

1. **Decide whether the collective nouns in the following sentences should have singular or plural verbs. Some may be correct as they stand.**

   a. The board has voted themselves a raise at yesterday's meeting.

   b. The congregation is shaving their beards.

   c. Each member of the team takes turns cleaning out the locker room.

   d. The provincial government have closed these offices indefinitely.

   e. The class is receiving their grades today.

   f. Fish that are on the endangered species list should not appear on restaurant menus.

   g. The police in that precinct has been accused of brutality in the riot.

   h. A family often have certain genetic predispositions.

   i. The number of successful applicants was very low.

   j. A number of good suggestions was made by the students.

Name _____ Course _____ Date _____

U5. INCLUSIVE LANGUAGE. If you have problems completing this exercise, refer to page 159 of *A Canadian Writer's Guide*. Answers appear at the end of this workbook.

1. Edit the following sentences to eliminate inclusive language.

a. The foreman asked Weldon and Harold to work late on Thursday to complete an important order for an American client.

b. Lorne goes to a lady dentist who works especially with orthodontics.

c. An architect must be careful to listen carefully to his clients.

d. Mankind must take care to preserve its delicate relationship with mother nature.

e. The actress thanked her mother and manager as she accepted her award.

f. After the new premier takes office, he must organize his advisors.

g. The waitress spilled soup all over her boss.

h. The boss asked if she would be willing to man the phone lines.

i. To become a policeman, you need considerable training.

j. Has the mailman arrived yet?

Name _____ Course _____ Date _____

U7. ACTIVE AND PASSIVE VOICE. If you have problems completing this exercise, refer to page 163 of *A Canadian Writer's Guide*. Answers appear at the end of this workbook.

1. Change any passive-voice clauses into the active voice.

a. Funds are raised by the board of governors for special events at the Royal Botanical Gardens.

b. The radical faction of the party was represented by a demure, young woman named Phoebe.

c. Grave mistakes were made by the company's negotiating team at this year's salary meeting.

d. In the hit TV show *24*, Jack Bauer is played by Canadian actor Kiefer Sutherland.

e. In the topic sentence, the paragraph's subject is concisely conveyed.

f. The tobacco companies were alarmed by the new anti-smoking legislation.

g. At the national boxing championships, the former champion was knocked out by a newcomer in the fifth round.

h. A disappointing prom night is experienced by a lot of high schoolers every June.

i. The South Asian countries affected by the tsunami disaster were offered millions of dollars in aid by Canadians.

j. The construction engineer was offered a new position with a rival firm.

Name _____ Course _____ Date _____

2. Change any passive-voice clauses into the active voice.

a. The employees were poorly paid for their labour as the company's income statement clearly shows.

_____

b. All the assignments were submitted by the students on the final day of classes.

_____

c. A new set of financial statements was released by Nortel Communications.

_____

d. Her condition was diagnosed by Dr. Fong as chronic fatigue syndrome.

_____

e. The airplane crash was blamed on pilot error brought about by fatigue.

_____

f. Many misconceptions about the films are corrected in the latest study of Hitchcock's work.

_____

g. *Spider-Man 2* was seen by everybody who enjoyed the first *Spider-Man*.

_____

h. Sonny Liston was knocked out by the first round by Cassius Clay in February, 1964.

_____

i. The MP3 player was used by the spy to store files he downloaded from the company's server.

_____

j. The crowd at the AA hockey game was taken over by ruffians.

_____

Name _____ Course _____ Date _____

PUNCTUATION

P1. THE COMMA. If you have problems completing this exercise, refer to pages 207-211 of *A Canadian Writer's Guide.* Answers appear at the end of this workbook.

1. **Add or remove commas where necessary in the following sentences. Some sentences may be correct as they stand.**

    a. Whatever is bothering you in your personal life is none of his affair.

    b. Sri Lanka Thailand and Indonesia suffered immense devastation and loss of life when a tsunami struck the Indian Ocean.

    c. People who want everything are greedy materialists.

    d. Karl Jacobs, who was a fan of conventional 35mm film cameras, was sceptical about buying a digital camera for his trip to Italy.

    e. The lights were lowered and a quiet hush descended over the audience.

    f. Although some believe that children's books are juvenile others recognize the depth of the material.

    g. Regardless of how much money you want to make you have to make it ethically.

    h. The people whom you love most have the most power to hurt you.

    i. If you had listened to me in the first place this disaster would not have happened.

    j. Bryan Adams best known as one of the most popular Canadian rock singers and performers is now considered one of the best portrait photographers in the world.

2. Add or remove commas where necessary in the following sentences. Some sentences may be correct as they stand.

a. As she answered the door Jamie Lee thought of all the horror movies she had seen in her life.

b. There is in fact no evidence to support the charges of corruption against the city councillor.

c. Instead of drinking wine I now imbibe club soda.

d. The pearls in the garage sale were sold immediately but she hadn't meant to put them out with the costume jewellery.

e. Yes there are a number of ways to sell your products online.

f. Mr. Deeds you don't realize what you are asking!

g. I cannot understand how in a world so reliant on technology she can live without having a telephone.

h. What your mother thinks of my apartment, doesn't concern me.

i. Jason was about to take a shower after his workout, but changed his mind.

j. Good manners suggest, therefore that you use your napkin to wipe your hands.

Name _____ Course _____ Date _____

P2 AND P3. THE SEMICOLON AND THE COLON. If you have problems completing this exercise, refer to pages 211-213 of *A Canadian Writer's Guide.* Answers appear at the end of this workbook.

1. **Edit the following sentences, using the semicolon and the colon correctly. Some sentences may be correct as they stand.**

   a. Mary's grocery list always included: cat food and magazines.

   b. The contributions came from: Canada, the USA, France, Germany and England.

   c. Several streets had to be renamed after the city amalgamated two of its boroughs, including the following; Dorchester, Church, and Pine.

   d. Marian was shocked when Li told everyone she had she'd failed the chemistry mid-term: she thought she could trust Li to keep a secret.

   e. The coaches' advice proved correct: the team played better than ever but still lost.

   f. The campers could not stand the weather; which was no wonder because the air was cold, and the mosquitoes were troublesome.

   g. Ansel decided to take pictures only of landscapes; dramatic, unique, colourful landscapes.

   h. The students bought books; papers; and printer cartridges.

   i. Dennis tried everything to get her attention, including: shouting and running back and forth.

   j. Nancy wore gumboots; a slicker; and her warmest mittens.

Name _____ Course _____ Date _____

P3. REVIEW OF THE SEMICOLON, THE COLON, AND THE COMMA. If you have problems completing this exercise, refer to pages 207-212 of *A Canadian Writer's Guide*. Answers appear at the end of this workbook.

1. **Edit the following paragraph, adding commas, semicolons, or colons where indicated by the square brackets.**

The way of life for many Canadians is changing[ ]but does anybody know what that really means? In Saskatchewan[ ] for example[ ] farmers have been abandoning their land in droves over the past ten years. In 1990[ ] rural municipalities accounted for 20 percent of Saskatchewan's population[ ] by the end of the decade, however, they were only 15 percent. Numbers[ ] of course[ ] tell only part of the story. People are moving away from the rural areas to cities like Calgary and Edmonton[ ] and the small towns that serviced them are shrinking and dying. In just another decade places such as Mendham[ ] Eastend[ ] and Swift Current will be completely unpopulated. Houses will stand empty[ ] and stores[ ] businesses[ ] and churches that once bustled with people will have locked their doors permanently. The prairie towns are disappearing and are taking with them a part of Canada's heritage.

2. **Edit the following paragraph, adding commas, semicolons, or colons where indicated by the square brackets.**

Residents of the town of Mendham[ ] Saskatchewan[ ] have one piece of advice for anyone wanting to pay their town a visit[ ] Hurry up before its gone! This is because the town's population has been decreasing rapidly over the past decade[ ] in a few years[ ] it may become only a name on the map of southern Saskatchewan. However[ ] life in Mendham has not always been this way. The town was once a centre of activity and boasted the following[ ] a bowling alley[ ] a pool hall[ ] five service stations[ ] a lumberyard[ ] a car dealership[ ] three churches[ ] and three grocery stores. There is[ ] perhaps[ ] no better illustration of the decline of rural life than the field on the outskirts of the town[ ] on it lie the rusting remains of dozens of tractors. These machines[ ] once a vital part of the area's livelihood[ ] are themselves now harvested for their spare parts.

Name _____ Course _____ Date _____

3. Edit the following paragraph, adding commas, semicolons, or colons where indicated by the square brackets.

Small town life across Canada is permanently changing. Often[ ] however[ ] the forces of change are government policy instead of economic factors. Half a century ago[ ] there were about 1[ ]200 settlements in Newfoundland. The inhabitants of these tiny villages fished the ocean for their livelihood[ ] and many of them built the houses they lived in. The towns had names as colourful as some of the characters that lived in them. For example[ ] have you ever heard of Ireland's Eye[ ] Indian Burying Place[ ] or Great Paradise? The harsh climate and decades of neglect have reduced these towns to piles of rotting lumber.

4. Edit the following paragraph, adding commas, semicolons, or colons where indicated by the square brackets.

Along 10[ ]000 kilometres of Newfoundland's coastline are the remnants of over a thousand fishing villages. The residents of these towns left their homes not because they could no longer fish the oceans[ ] they left because they were paid to leave. Joey Smallwood[ ] the premier of Newfoundland at the time[ ] had a vision[ ] move people from these tiny "outports" to several centres of economic growth. Once there[ ] these people would work in modern fisheries or factories that the premier hoped industrialists would erect. Few of these facilities were ever built[ ] however[ ] for more than forty years[ ] the federal and provincial governments paid more than 28[ ]000 people to move from the old settlements. Some were happy to leave the poor conditions in these towns[ ] others were more reluctant and felt that they were little more than pieces in a game played by the government.

P5. APOSTROPHES. If you have problems completing this exercise, refer to pages 217-219 of *The Canadian Writer's Guide*. Answers appear at the end of this workbook

1. **Add or remove apostrophes where needed in the following sentences. Some sentences may be correct as they stand.**

    a. The babies baths were too hot for tender skin.
    b. This candys taste reminds me of spiced apples.
    c. The police hadnt anticipated the sprays effect before using in on the suspect.
    d. The class spirit lifted when they discovered theyd be allowed to rewrite the test.
    e. Professor Bohrs began every class by reciting the students names.
    f. They say that Saturdays child is full of grace.
    g. The three weeks sale is over.
    h. The cats flea collar was around its neck.
    i. The Smiths party was the best, better even than our's.
    j. The Niagara Falls ride was really thrilling.

2. **Add or remove apostrophes where needed in the following sentences. Some sentences may be correct as they stand.**

    a. The hunters time is wasted if their luck is bad.
    b. In January, mens and womens coats were on sale for half the regular price.
    c. It's eyes glowed eerily in the moons waning light.
    d. Bess dress was a bright blue, which matched her eye's.
    e. We thought the agents reports were missing until we realized theyd given them to the enemy.
    f. Conrad brought an album of U2s greatest hits to Charles part on Saturday.
    g. In many large cities, citizens groups have been formed to prevent crime.
    h. Harry has always loved his mother-in-laws cooking more than his wifes.
    i. Their's was not a happy home but neither was ours'.
    j. Mr. James is waiting for the train sets to go on sale before hell buy one for his sons.

Name _____ Course _____ Date _____

P5. OTHER PUNCTUATION MARKS. If you have problems completing this exercise, refer to pages 219-221 of *A Canadian Writer's Guide*. Answers appear at the end of this workbook.

1. Edit the following sentences to correct errors in punctuation, focusing especially on correct use of the dash, the slash, parentheses, and quotation marks.

a. Jim Carrey perhaps the most famous Canadian actor lived a life of poverty while growing up in Toronto.

b. Who knows the poem My Funny Valentine?

c. My son's only two, but he knows the words to Baa, Baa Black Sheep.

d. Jason wrote a poem called Water Towers, which was about the industrial neighbourhood he grew up in now completely transformed by development.

e. Myron's hobbies photography and music are among the most expensive anyone could ever have.

f. It's a small price to pay for ensuring happiness and mental health he often says.

g. Essential oils of which Omega 3 is the best-known are derived mostly from fish mackerel, shark and especially cod.

h. Neighbours called him knucklehead not because he was stupid indeed, he had a Ph.D. in astrophysics but because rode an antique Harley-Davidson motorcycle made famous by its knuckle-shaped cylinder heads.

i. Do you realize, she said, how much money we've spent on this car lately?

j. Look up the word irregardless in the dictionary.

P6 PUNCTUATION REVIEW. Answers appear at the end of this workbook.

1. Edit the following paragraph, adding or removing punctuation where necessary.

Inquiry as a form of learning is useful to allow people to find real answers to problems they pose themselves and to learn how to do research not just in the library in traditional fashion but with others through interviews surveys and discussion or reflection. Inquiry is useful to survey a field or to allow the creative input of those involved in a particular subject area. The teacher can coach students but essentially the object is for learners to teach themselves as they go along with some monitoring from the teacher and assistance from others perhaps in group situations.

Inquiry is not directed by the teacher but instead by the learner. Students learn to be independent and they frame questions and solutions for themselves. When all the resources are widely dispersed inquiry is especially useful to explore new areas. In an inquiry course such as Topics in Multimedia students work in groups to explore questions about censorship on the Internet and the value of the Internet for education. They learn research skills and find a number of resources not known to any of us before. The nature of Internet research itself leads to this kind of open-ended research, it helps students find their feet in research situations in which they need to frame their own answerable clear questions and solutions to them.

Name _____ Course _____ Date _____

2. Edit the following paragraph, adding or removing punctuation where necessary.

Students as a general rule use study questions as the basis for their learning do workshops on Internet research and learn how to conduct group discussions which are intended to help them accomplish their goals. We "contract" with each other that is we have a schedule of presentations and due dates for final reports when the group will submit one assignment. Participation, on a regular basis is also an essential part of the contract.

Inquiry teaching does not lead a student through course material, in fact the students to a large extent find their own course material. Courses are in most cases divided into cycles; the students meet in groups to decide on a topic, then they gather information, then they work to synthesize, and finally they present it to the rest of the group, and submit a report to the teacher. Students are taught research skills and writing skills; helped to select workable topics; and given guidelines for their presentations and reports.

Inquiry teaching requires a lot of trust, teachers don't go in to class with an agenda or a lecture prepared. They go in with perhaps a small lesson on research methods, but mostly with an eye to watching over groups as they meet, and discuss their topics. Teachers do a lot of monitoring, and almost no "front of the class" teaching.

Name _____ Course _____ Date _____

MECHANICS

M2. Capitalization. If you have problems completing this exercise, refer to pages 235-237 of *A Canadian Writer's Guide*. Answers appear at the end of this workbook.

1. **Identify errors in the use of capitalization in the following sentences. Some sentences may be correct as they stand.**

    a. When Columbus reached the west indies in 1492, he thought he'd reached india.

    b. The king of france sent Jacques cartier to what is now Canada in order to find wealth, claim land and explore the gulf of st. lawrence.

    c. Joel Bakan's book, *the corporation: the pathological pursuit of profit and power*, was a bestseller and was turned into an award-winning documentary.

    d. Florence thought that *the chicago manual of style* was a home decorating book.

    e. Little did she know that the book could only help her with her English grammar, not with helping her to choose paint colours.

    f. French, italian and romanian are all derived from latin, which was spread throughout the european continent by roman soldiers over 2000 years ago.

    g. It is important for Professors to understand that their muslim students will probably experience fatigue in class during ramadan, the holy month of fasting.

    h. A robotic probe launched from earth two years ago finally landed on titan, the largest of jupiter's moons.

    i. Abu dubai, which is the Capital City of the united arab emirates, is a popular destination for shoppers around the world because no one pays import and export duties.

    j. You can't find anywhere in History a better example of musical genius than the beach boys.

Name _____ Course _____ Date _____

M3. Abbreviations. If you have problems completing this exercise, refer to pages 238-240 of *A Canadian Writer's Guide*. Answers appear at the end of this workbook.

1. **Edit the following exercises to correct errors in abbreviations. Some sentences may be correct as they stand.**

   a. Sitting in the auditorium with hundreds of other students, Janice found her intro. psych. class intimidating.

   b. The markets in the U.S. have been plummeting lately.

   c. Economic indicators in the U.S. do not look very promising these days.

   d. Dr. Nathaniel Ostermann was my biology prof. for two years.

   e. This year Xmas will fall on a Wed.

   f. Worldvision, Care and Unicef helped to organize aid to those countries stricken by the earthquake and tsunami in the Indian Ocean.

   g. The Dr. who specializes in back injuries examined Mortimer after he fell from the ladder at work.

   h. Despite an improving regional economy, PEI will always be Canada's smallest province.

   i. The U.S. political strategy in the Middle East is troubling to many Canadians.

   j. Canada has many diplomatic connections with the UK.

Name _____ Course _____ Date _____

M4. NUMBERS. If you have problems completing this exercise, refer to pages 241-243 of *A Canadian Writer's Guide*. Answers appear at the end of this workbook.

1. Edit the following sentences to correct errors in the use of numbers. Some sentences may be correct as they stand.

a. About 4 years ago, Martin and Laura had their 2nd child, and after that their lives have never been the same.

_____

_____

b. Our sixth wedding anniversary is on Sunday, February 27.

_____

c. We intend to purchase four three-door filing cabinets for the new office.

_____

d. $120 is what I paid to have the brakes on my Italian racing bicycle repaired.

_____

e. After his 3rd divorce, Tom went to China and started his life over.

_____

f. With 75 students and only 1 teacher, this class has a 75:1 student-teacher ratio.

_____

g. 11 MLAs from some of the most important ridings urged Premier Klein to run for a 4th term in office.

_____

h. Act I, scene 1 of *Macbeth* introduces the 3 witches.

_____

i. The amount that the Canadian government pledge to relief efforts totalled $425,000,000.

_____

j. The two new parking lots at the mall should provide space for an additional 330 cars.

_____

_____

64   M4 *Numbers*

Name _____ Course _____ Date _____

M5. HYPHENS. If you have problems completing this exercise, refer to pages 243-245 of *A Canadian Writer's Guide.* Answers appear at the end of this workbook.

1. Identify errors in the use of hyphens in the following sentences. Some sentences may be correct as they stand.

   a. Today is my forty ninth birthday.

   b. My father thinks he's getting his money's worth if dines at an all you can eat buffet.

   c. My brother in law was seriously injured when he slipped on a puddle in the grocery-store.

   d. The bridge was only six years old when it first needed repairs.

   e. The Lieutenant Governor and the Governor General attended the opening of the hospital's new wing.

   f. James was the self-appointed leader of the book club.

   g. My Member-of-Parliament intervened on our behalf to halt construction of the new housing development.

   h. Well-known author and singer, Vic Dane appeared at the Limelight Club on Saturday.

   i. Highly-developed self-esteem is something many excellent public speakers possess.

   j. One fifth of all respondents said that they did not care who ran the offshore oil well.

ANSWERS

BASIC GRAMMAR

B1 Identifying Parts of Speech

1. page 1
   a. life = 1, rain = 1, must fall = 3.
   b. picture = 1, words = 1, is = 3
   c. has got = 3, cat = 1, your = 2, tongue = 1
   d. stitch = 1, time = 1, saves = 3, nine = 1
   e. dies = 3, swan = 1
   f. fences = 1, make = 3, neighbours = 1
   g. fool = 1, his = 2, money = 1, are parted = 3
   h. seeing = 1, is = 3, believing =1
   i. count = 3, your = 2, chickens = 1, they = 2, hatch = 3
   j. talk = 1, is = 3

2. page 1
   a. a = 5, saved = 1, a = 5, earned = 1
   b. together = 2, together = 2
   c. before = 2
   d. when = 2, the = 5, away = 5
   e. and = 3
   f. by = 4
   g. the = 5, in = 4, mainly = 2, on = 4, the = 5
   h. a = 5, rolling = 1, no = 2
   i. the = 5, of = 4
   j. a = 5, watched = 1, never = 2

3. page 2
   a. executives = 1, spend = 3, their = 2
   b. you = 2, deal = 3, cards = 2, you = 2, should be = 3
   c. picture = 1, my = 2, book = 1, was = 3, mass = 1, green = 1, blue = 1.
   d. picture = 3, beach = 1, trees = 1
   e. shirt = 1, one = 1, fibre = 1, fabrics = 1 is = 3, can breathe = 3
   f. silk = 1, is = 3, cotton = 1
   g. manual labour = 1, is becoming = 3
   h. reading = 1, manual = 1, is = 3, trial = 1, those = 2, us = 2, who = 2, are = 3 technology = 1
   i. officer =1, will book = 3, driver = 1
   j. librarians = 1, me = 2, believe = 3, book = 1, is = 3, commodity =1

4. page 2
   a. a = 5, new = 1, how = 2
   b. by = 4, a = 5, than = 2, in = 4, and = 3

   c. the = 5, of = 4, Chinese = 1, and = 3, English = 1, differently = 2
   d. previously = 2, even = 2, in = 4, different = 1, same = 1, biological = 1
   e. many = 1, the = 5, in = 4, the = 5, left = 1, temporal = 1, of = 4, the = 5
   f. most = 1, at = 4, alphabetic = 1, like = 4, English = 1, and = 3, Italian = 1,
   g. however = 3, more = 2, heavily = 3, on = 4, in = 4, written = 1
   h. magnetic = 1, resonance = 1, imaging = 1, on = 4, Chinese = 1, with = 4, how = 2, when = 2
   i. a = 5, completely = 2, different = 1, of = 4, the = 5, in = 4, the = 5, impaired = 1, Chinese = 1, than = 3, in = 4, English = 1
   j. the = 5, the = 5, of = 4, to = 4, in = 4, when = 3, very = 3, complicated = 2

B2 Identifying Phrases

1. page 4
   a. of Alberta = 1, Ralph Klein = 5, in office = 1
   b. smoking cigarettes = 3
   c. to live dangerously = 4
   d. given the enormous cost of living in the city = 6
   e. eaten cold = 2
   f. in the coffee pot = 1, for an extra cup = 1
   g. sitting in my lap = 3
   h. Diane and Lena = 5, dancing at nightclubs = 3
   i. tears streaming down her face = 6
   j. into arguments = 1, over money = 1

2. page 4
   a. living well = 3
   b. asleep at the wheel = 2, off the road = 1
   c. one eye open = 6, at me = 1, from across the pillow = 1
   d. tired after a hard day's work = 2, into the tub = 1
   e. a sports car and a BMW = 5, in the driveway = 1
   f. to be honest = 4, in a million years = 1
   g. to have been part of the Olympics = 4, for the gymnast = 1
   h. having a manicure = 3
   i. winning the lottery = 3, from my mind = 1
   j. to dance the night away = 4

3. page 5

    The International Friends [of Literature = 1] is an organization [dedicated {to the creation =1} {of peace = 1} {through culture and literature= 1} =2]. It was founded [in 1985= 1] [in Haifa, Israel = 1] and registered [as a voluntary association =1] [in 1987.= 1] This organization strives [to illustrate how important it is= 4] [to analyze fictional tales= 4] [of war and violence= 1] [when researching peace =2]. [Studying literature = 3] is an important part [of peace research= 1] because it enables individuals [to examine the different values= 4] [of peace studies= 1] [in a variety = 1] [of situations,= 1] thus [helping = 3] [to reinforce many of the key concepts = 4] [of peace = 1] [In fiction,= 1] the values [of peace = 1] and the destructiveness [of war = 1] are presented [in a way = 1] that allows researchers [to explore alternative methods = 4] [to achieve conflict resolution = 4] [without endorsing or rejecting methods = 1] uncritically. [As a result =1], literature may have a decisive role [in shaping peace processes. = 2]

B2 Constructing Clauses

1. page 6
   a. After considering how she was treated, Denise decided to quit her job as the assistant manager.
   b. The iPod, an MP3 player, has become one of the most popular electronic gadgets in recent years.
   c. Fixing something is difficult when you do not have the right tools.
   d. To find a rewarding job is the greatest challenge that students face today.
   e. During the summer, electricity use usually rises because people turn on their air conditioners.
   f. Mrs. Lupinski, the woman who broke her leg last week, showed up to the wedding in a formal gown and crutches.
   g. Remote control in hand, Tito collapsed on the couch and slept until noon the next day.
   h. Karim disliked having to get used to new surroundings when he moved from his home in Kenya.
   i. Working part-time to pay for tuition is a reality that more Canadian students are facing.
   j. When he saw his friends receiving rewards for their artistic accomplishments, Jeremy began to regret the fact that he didn't take more risks in his life.

B2 Identifying Clauses

1. page 7

North Americans are fat and getting fatter. = 1 Two out of three Americans are overweight or obese, = 1 and recent Canadian studies show the same trends developing here. = 1 When two teenage girls in the United States sued McDonald's for making them obese, = 2 documentary filmmaker Morgan Spurlock set out to discover what has made people so fat. = 1 The result is his film *Super Size Me*, = 1 a hilarious and often shocking look at the effects of fast food on the human body. = 2

Spurlock conducted an experiment. = 1 He would subject himself to a diet of nothing but McDonald's fast food for 30 days. = 1 He allowed himself to eat only what was available over the counter at the restaurant. = 1 He had to eat every item on the McDonald's menu at least once, = 1 and he had to eat breakfast, lunch, and dinner every day. = 1 Throughout his experiment, = 2 he visited doctors and health professionals to track his decline in health. = 1 At the beginning of the film, = 2 Spurlock measured 6' 2" tall and weighed 185 pounds. = 1 His cholesterol was a healthy 168, his blood pressure 120/80, and his body fat measured 11%. = 1 A month later, = 2 Spurlock's weight had shot up to 210 pounds, his cholesterol was 230, and body fat had increased to 18%. = 1

Super Size Me uses humour to present a harsh condemnation of the practices used to lure people, = 1 especially children, into eating fast food. = 2 McDonald's sets itself up for exactly the kind of lawsuit it was subjected to = 1 simply because of its targeting of children with clowns, "happy meals," and cartoons. = 2 The film ends, however, by reporting that the two teenage girls failed in their lawsuit against McDonald's = 1 and, shortly after, the United States Congress passed a law prohibiting people from suing fast food restaurants for obesity. = 1

2. page 8
Almost half of Ontario's adults are overweight, = 1 and measures need to be taken to reduce what has become an obesity "epidemic". = 1 These are the words of the province's chief medical officer in her annual report. = 1 Dr. Sheila Basrur said she was alarmed to find that almost one out of every two adults in Ontario is overweight or obese. = 1 The report also warns that obesity among children aged seven to 13 tripled between 1981 and 1996. = 1 In addition to contributing to heart disease, strokes, hypertentions and some forms of cancer, = 2 unhealthy weights are responsible for a dramatic rise in adult-onset diabetes. = 1 When combined with sensible eating habits, = 2 active living combined with sensible eating habits would improve the quality of life for everyone in the province. = 1

The report contains several recommendations for the Ontario government, = 1 including a mass-media campaign to increase awareness of the benefits of maintaining a healthy weight. = 2 Basrur also asked the government to control food advertising aimed at children, = 1 similar to measures in Quebec prohibiting advertising of some products to children under the age of 13. = 2 The report also suggests that the federal government act to phase out trans fat from processed foods and require large chain restaurants to disclose basic nutrition facts about the foods they serve. = 1 The report recommends that the food industry decrease serving sizes, = 1 especially of snack foods and increase the use of user-friendly food labelling on large chain restaurant menus and take-out foods. = 2 By taking steps to solve the problem of obesity now, = 2 we will hopefully be reducing the burden on the healthcare system in the future. = 1

SENTENCE ELEMENTS

S1 Identifying Parts of Sentences

1. page 9
    a. Ads [ads = SS} are the cave art of the twentieth century. —*Marshall McLuhan*
    b. The ideal companion [companion = SS} in bed is a good book. —*Robertson Davies*
    c. There is no blood [blood = SS]in our history. —*Pierre Berton*
    d. To write [To write = SS] simply is as difficult as to be good. —*Somerset Maugham*
    e. Writing [writing = SS] is turning one's worst moments into money. —*J.P. Donleavy*
    f. Writers, [writers = SS] like teeth, are divided into incisors and grinders. —*Walter Bagehot*

g. <u>To reveal art and conceal the artist</u> [To reveal and conceal = SS] is art's aim. —*Oscar Wilde*
   h. <u>A great many people now reading and writing</u> [people = SS] would be better employed keeping rabbits. —*Edith Sitwell*
   i. There are <u>books</u> [books = SS] of which the backs and covers are by far the best part. —*Charles Dickens*
   j. <u>The devil</u> [devil = SS] doesn't make personal appearances. —*Morris Panych*

2. page 10
   a. <u>Every vital development in language</u> [development = SS] is a development of feeling as well. —*T. S. Eliot*
   b. <u>My pencils</u> [pencils = SS] outlast their erasers. —*Vladmir Nabokov*
   c. <u>Words</u> [words = SS] pick up flavours and odours like butter in a refrigerator. —*John Steinbeck*
   d. Why shouldn't <u>we</u> [we = SS] quarrel about a word? —*G. K. Chesterton*
   e. <u>The art of writing</u> [art = SS] has for backbone some fierce attachment to an idea —*Virginia Woolf*
   f. <u>All good writing</u> [writing = SS] is swimming under water and holding your breath. —*F. Scott Fitzgerald*
   g. Better far write twaddle or anything, anything, than nothing at all. [You understood = SS] —*Katherine Mansfield*
   h. <u>Language</u> [language = SS] is the archives of history. —*Ralph Waldo Emerson*
   i. <u>A poet</u> [poet = SS] can survive everything but a misprint. —*Oscar Wilde*
   j. <u>I</u> [I = SS] believe in miracles in every area except writing. —*Isaac Bashevis Singer*

3. page 11
   a. If you can't do {*the time,*} [DO] don't do *the crime*. [DO] —*Earl Work*
   b. Give {*a man*} [IO] {*an inch*}[DO], and he thinks *he's a ruler*. [DO] —*Don Harron*
   c. Every writer is a frustrated actor who recites his *lines* [DO] in the hidden auditorium of his skull. —*Rod Serling*
   d. I wrote my first *novel* [DO] because I wanted to read *it*. [DO] —*Toni Morrison*
   e. He is the best orator who can turn men's *ears* into eyes. [DO]
   f. Writing fiction has become a priestly business in countries that have lost their *faith*. [DO] —*Gore Vidal*
   g. When you catch an *adjective,* [DO] kill *it*. [DO] —*Mark Twain*
   h. Quotation confesses *inferiority*. [DO] —*Ralph Waldo Emerson*
   i. Real art has the *capacity* [DO] to make us nervous. —*Susan Sontag*
   j. A little inaccuracy sometimes saves *tons* [DO] of explanations. —*Saki*

4. page 12
   a. No word was ever as effective as a *rightly timed pause* [OC]. —*Mark Twain*
   b. No human being can really understand *another,* [DO] and no one can arrange another's *happiness*. [DO] —*Graham Greene*

c. Art attempts to find in the universe, in matter as well as in the facts of life, *what is fundamental, enduring, essential.* [DO] —*Saul Bellow*
d. I'll make *him* [IO] an *offer* [DO] he can't refuse. —*Mario Puzo*
e. Parents are the bones on which children sharpen their *teeth*. [DO]
—*Peter Ustinov*
f. The true writer has *nothing* [DO] to say. —*Alain Robbe-Grillet*
g. If a man hasn't discovered *something that he will die for*, [DO] he isn't fit to live.
—*Martin Luther King*
h. Don't count your *chickens* [DO] before they hatch. – *English Proverb*
i. The prayer of the chicken hawk does not get *him* [IO] the *chicken*. [DO]
—*Swahili proverb*
j. The eggs do not teach the *hen*. [DO] —*Russian proverb*

S2 Identifying Sentence Patterns

1. page 13
    a. David and Maureen wrote their certification exam this morning. 3
    b. Dr. Davis regards homeopathic medicine a hoax. 5
    c. Garth seemed preoccupied today in class. 2
    d. She gave the clerk her passport. 4
    e. My professor wears the same jacket each Monday. 3
    f. The chain reaction is the basis of nuclear power. 2
    g. Mandy practices her violin daily. 3
    h. Doctors feel the discovery to be a breakthrough in treating depression. 5
    i. The firm is building children a new playground in the park. 4
    j. Prolonged exposure to the chemical can be fatal. 1

2. page 13
    a. The debating club elected Michael president. (5)
    b. The lab assistants ate five pizzas at their office Christmas party. (3)
    c. The telephone rings constantly. (1)
    d. The guidance counsellor gave me the best advice. (4)
    e. Some people consider musicals dull. (5)
    f. Lear will never forgive his daughters. (3)
    g. Hamlet hesitates too much. (1)
    h. Lady Macbeth gives her husband the motivation to murder the king. (4)
    i. *Titus Andronicus* shocks theatre audiences. (3)
    j. Shakespeare uses violence in many of his plays. (3)

S3 Identifying Sentence Types

1. page 14
    a. complex
    b. simple
    c. complex
    d. complex

    e. compound
    f. simple
    g. complex
    h. complex
    i. complex
    j. compound-complex

2. page 15
    a. simple
    b. compound
    c. compound
    d. complex
    e. compound-complex
    f. complex-complex
    g. simple
    h. complex
    i. simple
    j. complex

S5 Editing Sentences for Variety

1. page 16
Going back to school in September can be traumatic. For a student, it can be expensive, frustrating because the weather is still beautiful, and anxious because of new responsibilities. Trying to get used to a new schedule can be difficult, particularly if you have spent the summer sleeping in and taking advantage of the time off. Getting used to a new place of residence is also often challenging. Leaving the comfort and security of your parents' home can be a trial. School offers rewards to students: they get opportunities to meet new people and a chance to learn something new. Along with these new chances come many fears and pressures. To forget about the anxieties they feel, students need to appreciate the novelty of their lives. They can then discover September doesn't have to be a problem. Students who are organized will prosper, and those prepared to face change in their lives will find excitement and happiness.

2. page 17
This is the age of neuroscience. The human brain is a maze of wisdom, and we are finally exploring the home frontier in earnest. Much of this new data is due to the incredible tools we now have to investigate the human brain. CT scans and MRI machines make it possible for researchers to view changes in brain chemistry while the brain is in action. There are so many new findings coming out every day. Some are straightforward while others are controversial and even puzzling. For example, about a quarter of the brain is involved in visual processing; this is more than for all other senses. Because memory is most likely stored in the same areas of the brain that were involved in the perception, processing and analysis of the original input, scientists believe that there is not a single memory centre. Since it is a reactivation of the same neuronal circuit, the act of remembering is the re-experiencing of the original event. Finally, long thought

impossible, human neurogenesis has now been confirmed in some brain regions. This is the process of growing new brain cells, but we still do not know for certain what these new brain cells are for.

GRAMMATICAL SENTENCES

G1 Sentence Fragments

1. page 18
    a. There were many students working in Professor James's laboratory last summer.
    b. Do you think you are going to quit school? You will quit over my dead body.
    c. Ella liked living on the edge of the escarpment, which is why she dreaded having to leave her current job.
    d. Ilya, Enforcer being his role on the team, found himself spending a lot of time in the penalty box.
    e. David chose a cake for the party: the chocolate one that appealed to him the most.
    f. Having surrendered herself to the authorities, she was resigned to her fate.
    g. There were door prizes at the year-end party given by the organizers to entice people to show up.
    h. The programs run all year round with only a short break between each semester.
    i. You will soon be evicted, something which is just fine by me.
    j. Never in a million years believing her story, he stared at her in awe.

2. page 20
    a. I intend never in a million years to contact my former employer.
    b. Malcolm lay on the couch, digesting his dinner, for the rest of the night.
    c. Email is a great waste of time as many companies are finding out.
    d. Surely you are not—in this lifetime—going to quit your job.
    e. Correct.
    f. Working overtime is not always profitable because the taxes go up as well.
    g. Sleeping through the service, each of the Simpsons had a dream.
    h. Do not deny, not here, not now, your love for Sigismund.
    i. Solving exercises is easy whereas editing can be challenging.
    j. Although Laura has had a lot of experience as a dog trainer, she doesn't want to train dogs for a living.

G1 Run-on Sentences

1. page 21
    a. I may procrastinate; I don't quit though.
    b. The neighbour's dog overturned our garbage can. Then he scattered litter everywhere.
    c. Read the fine print on any contract before you sign. It could save you headaches later on.
    d. To be or not to be. That is the question.

e. Some people work to live; others live to work.
   f. I love you; you're perfect. Now change.
   g. Correct
   h. I know the answer. What was the question again?
   i. She's so stubborn. You can't argue with her.
   j. Correct

2. page 22
   a. There was no hockey on TV this year, so most people found something else to do.
   b. Life is a beach. I guess death is the deep end.
   c. Reality shows are inexpensive to produce; this is why there are so many on TV.
   d. I find contract work doesn't pay well; however, I need the money.
   e. Dog shows fascinate me; it doesn't matter which breed is best in show.
   f. You cannot base your life on what you see on TV shows. If you do you're headed for some bad news.
   g. Situation comedies are often about people over forty who are single and dating, but usually these shows don't bear much resemblance to life.
   h. It's ragweed season, and all my friends with allergies are sneezing.
   i. Gym glass was his nemesis since he lacked coordination and was always picked last for team sports.
   j. Cell phones are dangerous on the road; hence, drivers should use them only when parked.

G2 Subject-Verb Agreement

1. page 23
   a. There are two bottles of beer left in the cooler.
   b. A number of us are going to the carnival.
   c. Correct
   d. Edmund's favourite snack is pretzels and beer.
   e. Love and patience are required in the daycare centre.
   f. Neither he nor his friends have ever appeared on television.
   g. Each of the dogs wears a tag.
   h. There are two cars parked in the driveway.
   i. Neither Reneé nor the Johnsons have to wait for their awards now.
   j. Correct.

2. page 24
   a. Bits of angel food cake were always to be found on the kitchen floor.
   b. Items available for sale on ebay.ca are plentiful but sometimes of questionable quality.
   c. The presence of critics in the audience has always disturbed me during performances.
   d. Nearly everyone on the board approves of the latest pay increases.
   e. Neither management nor the players appear to be ready to make any concessions.
   f. At CBC the history of film and television in Canada comes alive.

g. Judie was the only one of my friends who insists that I should try harder.
h. The key concern of the committee members is the perks and the use of the free limousine.
i. Every year a number of fish with high level of Mercury are caught in that river.
j. Owning a house and a car has placed considerable stress on their marriage.

G2 Verb Tense and Mood Agreement

1. page 25
    a. One person hands out the brochure, and the other asks passersby if they would like more information about the service.
    b. The candidate for the position was very forthcoming. She gave too much information about why she was fired from her previous job to the interviewers.
    c. Correct
    d. Thanksgiving dinner at my parents' house usually ends the same way every year. We snack, eat dinner, and fall asleep on the couch.
    e. The last Usher concert was really great. I went with my friend, and we stood two feet away from the stage the whole time.
    f. In *Fifth Business*, Robertson Davies creates the town of Deptford from his memories of small-town Ontario. Similarly, Alice Munro creates Hanratty as a substitute for her hometown, Hanover, Ontario.
    g. Boxing day sales usually offer consumers a chance to save money, but they also give merchants an opportunity to clear out old merchandise.
    h. After the fire, the rescuers bandaged the cat and prepared to take it to a shelter. It meowed pitifully.
    i. We walked through the Toronto's deserted streets at night until, finally, we found the Hockey Hall of Fame.
    j. I open my lunch box. And there it is: another corned beef sandwich.

2. page 27
    a. The comedian tells a joke, and the audience laughs hysterically.
    b. Correct
    c. The actress opened the envelope. The winner was Sean Penn.
    d. Government policy demands a certain procedure for the applications. For instance, one always asks for the health card number first.
    e. She asked what my name was, and I said John.
    f. I have lived in this town since I was ten years old.
    g. The power went off because the storm is so fierce.
    h. You would have been shocked by what we saw yesterday.
    i. After scoring well on the first test, Michelle was convinced that she would pass the course with ease.
    j. In the novel *The Life of Pi*, Yann Martel retells the story of Noah's Ark.

G2 Pronoun-Antecedent Agreement

1. page 28
   a. No one knew what he or she might be expected to do.
   b. The audience clapped its hands and registered its approval.
   c. Correct
   d. Every company has its own way of interviewing new applicants.
   e. Employees should keep their personal email separate from their work messages.
   f. Those who wear a thong should have their head examined.
   g. If a people choose to room alone on the trip, they will still have to pay double occupancy.
   h. The board voted to give themselves a raise after they dealt with the grievances presented to them.
   i. Participants should select their songs prior to the competition deadline.
   j. My family have eccentric tastes, but they sure know how to put on a show.

2. page 29
   a. One of the students must give his or her oral presentations tomorrow in class.
   b. Why is the sea bass an endangered species? It is being overfished in certain parts of the world because it is considered a delicacy.
   c. None of us should have to give up our dreams.
   d. If anyone knows of the suspect's whereabouts, he or she should contact the police immediately.
   e. People pray that it's their lottery numbers that get picked every Friday night.
   f. Each of the women hoped that the courses she was taking would lead to employment.
   g. The crowd got out of control and stormed the barriers.
   h. I lent someone the videotapes, and that person passed them on to friends.
   i. Each member of the committee must submit his or her candidate for consideration by the end of the week.
   j. If drivers leave the scene of an accident, they will lose their licence.

G3 Unclear Pronoun Reference

1. page 30
   a. Sean told Liam that he should stay away from Sean's little brother.
   b. Denise quit school, and she is waiting on tables.
   c. Drunk drivers cause accidents that should not happen.
   d. In Georgian Bay, there is a three-month long tourist season.
   e. The favourite beer in Australia is Victoria Bitter.
   f. It is bad luck to walk under a ladder.
   g. The lamb followed Mary to school, an activity which was against the rule.
   h. She couldn't say goodbye to her aunt because her aunt was sick.
   i. A lack of rain greatly affects the growth of the crops in the spring.
   j. Ms. Fracus didn't know what to say when Tamecka asked her for a raise.

2. page 31
   a. The runner who made the team at the last minute ended up placing first at the meet.
   b. Many people believe that interviewing processes are unreliable unless a strict hiring policy is carried out.
   c. We thought that seats would be available at the last moment. Since the star of the show is so popular, our hope turned out to be unrealistic.
   d. I'd like to become an electrician because the job pays well.
   e. Since the tutorial leader could write so well, we had the opportunity to practice our skills.
   f. When Phillip put the car in the garage, the car had a bent fender.
   g. Brazilians speak Portuguese, not Spanish.
   h. Be sure to visit Harbourfront's skating rink where lessons are offered every weekday.
   i. If you are hungry, you can visit the snack bar, where snacks are available fresh and at a discount.
   j. I ate and drank only enough to keep from being hungry.

G3 Misplaced Modifiers

1. page 32
   a. Scratching each other's backs, the gorillas were observed by the tourists.
   b. He keeps an ashtray, which he seldom uses, on his desk.
   c. Correct.
   d. The children watched the crocodiles, enclosed by barbed wire in their natural habitat,
   e. The pills he swallowed came from this bottle.
   f. Last week the supervisor was informed that the work was completed
   g. Rhonda's hobby was building furniture, a pastime which she found relaxing.
   h. The press reported that this morning the building would be torn down.
   i. Hardly anyone knew the answer.
   j. Tom worked in the grocery store only for a year.

2. page 33
   a. George took his sister, wearing a pink skirt, to see the exhibition.
   b. From an old friend, Kim received a letter about a show on portrait making
   c. I hope that it won't rain on the weekend.
   d. After her supervisor questioned her for over an hour, the nurse admitted that she didn't know CPR as well as she should have.
   e. The last time he saw her, Patrick promised to quit smoking.
   f. The media accused the prime minister was accused of mishandling the campaign funds.
   g. The old pictures showed a woman eating an ice cream cone in bed.
   h. You will need to plant just one package of seeds.
   i. Answering questions in front of a jury can be nerve-racking.

j. The assailant was described as a tall man weighing approximately 150 pounds, with a black moustache.

G3 Dangling Modifiers

1. page 34
    a. When using a drill, you require caution.
    b. To succeed in school, you may find a great deal of reading is necessary.
    c. Waking up early in the morning, I believe a cold shower is invigorating.
    d. Because I am facing baldness, his new medication is vital to me.
    e. Eating some sticky candy, he found that his braces got stuck.
    f. Raising the interest rates adversely affected the market.
    g. As a new employee, I didn't think that the probationary period seemed threatening.
    h. To prevent food poisoning, one should not take mayonnaise on picnics.
    i. After criticizing my efforts, my boss fired me.
    j. She found the body while working on the night shift.

2. page 35
    a. Answering the phone, the babysitter shuddered.
    b. After we left the ship, the strange birds were the first things we noticed.
    c. Because she was a comedian at heart, her students often laughed during her class.
    d. After the student looked at all the examples, the math questions suddenly became easier.
    e. Correct.
    f. Although overwhelmed with credit card debt, Michael still found the leather chair irresistible.
    g. While looking for my purse, I was asked by a security guard asked if he could be of service.
    h. After she dieted rigorously for over six months, Mrs. Jones's husband thought his wife looked divinely slim.
    i. Burnt severely by the sun, he was relieved when a tube of ointment took away some of the pain.
    j. Sitting on the balcony, the happy tourists heard the sound of the surf.

G3 Faulty Parallel Structure

1. page 36
    a. Either you vacate the premises, or I call the police.
    b. Having practiced, prayed and trained hard, the Richview Scots football team placed first in the provincial competition.
    c. Having done all the chapter exercises, studied the review sheets, and memorized all the formulas, Henry knew he'd pass the final exam.
    d. People who believe in astrology are frequently dismissed as gullible, superstitious, and vain.

e. Dr. Shulman attributes his financial success to careful planning, keeping up with current events, and having a wealthy wife.
f. Mahatma Ghandi was the inspiration of many 20th century leaders because of his ability to perceive the root of a problem, to encourage others to support him, and to find non-violent methods of change.
g. The assistant's work included writing, teaching, and editing his papers carefully because his supervisor saw them.
h. When I changed the oil every 6 000 kilometres, the car seemed to run much better.
i. We regret not being able to ship the order at once and ask you to be patient.
j. In both western and eastern countries, there are concerns about economic development.

2. page 38
   a. Ethel finds it harder to be critical of others than to be critical of herself.
   b. My work involves teaching, marking papers, and constantly looking for a better job.
   c. Being a foreigner, not speaking the language, and being all alone, Freda decided to join a guided tour of Banff.
   d. The mentor's job is to help you fix your papers, write more skilfully, and understand your assignments better.
   e. At the pottery exhibit, we saw potters make ashtrays, dishes, bowls, and vases. They also painted finished items.
   f. The summer we went to England, we saw many plays, ate out a lot, and took a boat down the Thames.
   g. How much quieter it is to live in Dundas than in the downtown core of the city.
   h. The family decided to rent a cottage in the Lakes Region and allowed Bianca and I to use it for a month.
   i. Driver education teaches students to become better drivers by obeying traffic laws, never exceeding speed limits, and always watching the road signs.
   j. Correct.

USAGE AND DICTION

U1 Redundancy and Wordiness

1. page 39
   a. This printer produces four pages per minute.
   b. The desire to express oneself is a universal craving that.
   c. The widespread use of narcotics has created other problems such as crime and the spread of diseases.
   d. Toronto's international airport is located close to the city.
   e. Your van has been repaired and can be picked up whenever you wish.
   f. Downtown, the project manager planned to operate round-the-clock.
   g. I think that the cheque should be returned to the customer.

    h. We attach our statement for $500 for services from May through August.
    i. If you repair your SUV, you should secure an estimate first.
    j. The senate decided that it agreed with my boss's proposal to terminate my position indefinitely.

2. page 41
    a. Your job will be to prepare all information received by every employee within the precinct.
    b. I will quit as soon as I can..
    c. Her new outfit consisted of a red dress, which she wore with a lambswool sweater.
    d. Jobs have become more and more difficult to find for new graduates.
    e. Because she is older than I am, my parents trusted her judgement more than mine.
    f. Your charge card is enclosed; you will find it a great convenience while shopping at any one of our stores.
    g. The end of the corridor terminates at a small green door.
    h. The first time Sheila failed her driver's test, she realized she would have to slow down the next time around.
    i. The current main concern of the board is whether the president has the ability to continue.
    j. On September 3rd, the Premier officially opened the east wing of the Hospital for Sick Children.

U1 Appropriate Connotations and Slang

1. page 43
    a. Seventy-five percent of North American households have vehicles of some kind in their possession.
    b. Regardless of her political problems in the past, Kim Campbell now holds a prestigious position.
    c. You have to be assertive when driving in the Montreal.
    d. The chauffeur was severely criticized for his part in the fatal accident.
    e. Symptoms of influenza include sore throat, coughing, headache, and vomiting.
    f. After being refused a reprieve, the prisoner ate his last meal and waited for the execution.
    g. The Leafs fans were disappointed when their team lost in the playoffs again.
    h. Students are encouraged to communicate with their advisors at least weekly.
    i. Theckla wasn't happy when she found out she had badly failed the physics final exam.
    j. Students who perform well on the examination will be assured of a good final grade.

2. page 44
    a. Tuition is expensive, but it will not be exorbitant if students prepare for their education carefully.

- b. The authorities have decreed that no one may drink in this province until the age of nineteen.
- c. The marketing teacher reprimanded Oswald in front of the whole class for talking on his cell phone.
- d. Municipal governments have raised the rates of property owners to collect more taxes.
- e. These days, young people need to be careful about their exposure to drugs.
- f. Drivers who drink beyond a certain limit could face charges.
- g. Another 500 employees got laid off at Nortel Communications this week
- h. Tupac Shakur was killed in a drive by shooting in Las Vegas.
- i. Warren Buffet and Bill Gates have profited greatly in their respective professions and are among the richest people in the world.
- j. The criminal admitted his guilt in the robbery and was sentenced to jail.

U1 Clichés

1. page 45
   - a. The professor answered questions on general relativity with ease.
   - b. Denise could be very stubborn when it came to choosing paint colours for the house.
   - c. After hearing Stephen Lewis speak about the crisis in Africa, I decided act on his suggestions.
   - d. Herman's explanation of the theory of communicative action was convoluted.
   - e. After winning a second term in office, President Bush has found it easier to stay committed to his policies.
   - f. Hume's *Treatise Concerning Human Understanding* is not very exciting reading.
   - g. I have to leave for school at sunrise on Tuesdays and Thursdays.
   - h. There is little opposition to the new administration.
   - i. If your voice is hoarse, it's probably best to keep quiet.
   - j. Listen to me: There will be no make up test for this chapter.

U1 Idioms

1. page 46
   - a. The general public did not want to abide by the decision of the Supreme Court.
   - b. Be sure to answer all the questions completely before turning the page.
   - c. I intend to marry Dexter as soon as the divorce is final.
   - d. Why do you think white collar crime should be treated differently from fraud or embezzlement?
   - e. The look on her face showed that she was angry with her brother.
   - f. If you will try to come up with some answers to these questions, we may release you more quickly.
   - g. Her sister was envious of her new dishwasher.
   - h. Lance could not gather the courage to ask her on a date.
   - i. What type of a person do you think I am?
   - j. Work is preferable to prison.

U2 Pronoun Case

1. page 47
    a. Between you and me, I couldn't believe that the Americans had re-elected George W. Bush for President.
    b. Correct
    c. The blame must be accepted by you and me.
    d. Correct
    e. The amateur plays hockey better than he.
    f. What were you and she talking about?
    g. The supervisor asked Frances and me to work overtime.
    h. We are the only ones who should take the exam: my brother and I.
    i. The police officer gave the parking ticket to my husband and me.
    j. Cathy and we ate all the cake at the birthday party.

2. page 47
    a. The professor asked her and me to show our work to the rest of the class.
    b. He and his dad run the whole business together.
    c. The employment equity policy will affect her more than me.
    d. Correct
    e. Correct
    f. Correct
    g. That was he on MuchMusic the other night.
    h. My wife weighs ten pounds more than I.
    i. They speak Spanish better than we.
    j. Only two people were interviewed: Larry and I.

U3 Pronoun Choice

1. page 48
    a. Correct
    b. Daniel could not remember whom he'd given the papers to.
    c. We have met the lawyer whom you were speaking of.
    d. There is no one in the room who does not know the answer.
    e. Who do you think will answer the summons?
    f. Whoever told you that was wrong?
    g. He is someone who I believe always tells the truth.
    h. James, whom I consider an ally, advised me to take this action.
    i. Correct
    j. Whom do you think is likely to win the next *Canadian Idol*

2. page 48
    a. The group that I belong to is not political
    b. That group that I joined on the weekend is dedicated to weight loss
    c. Correct

d. Correct
   e. That yoga position that I learned yesterday is very difficult to sustain without practice.
   f. Correct.
   g. The DVD player that I bought only last year is already obsolete.
   h. Most DVD players that are available today can play MP3s, music files that are compressed to save space on a disc.
   i. The house that she owns is badly in need of repair.
   j. Cooking, which is a useful skill, should be taught in every high school.

U4 Agreement and Collective Nouns

1. page 49
   a. The board have voted themselves a raise at yesterday's meeting.
   b. The congregation are shaving their beards.
   c. Correct
   d. The provincial government has closed these offices indefinitely.
   e. The class are receiving their grades today.
   f. Fish that is on the endangered species list should not appear on restaurant menus.
   g. The police in that precinct have been accused of brutality in the riot.
   h. A family often has certain genetic predispositions.
   i. Correct.
   j. A number of good suggestions were made by the students.

U5 Inclusive Language

1. page 50
   a. The superviser asked Weldon and Harold to work late on Thursday to complete an important order for an American client.
   b. Lorne goes to a dentist who works especially with orthodontics.
   c. An architect must be careful to listen carefully to his or her clients.
   d. Humankind must take care to preserve its delicate relationship with nature.
   e. The actor thanked her mother and manager as she accepted her award
   f. After the new premier takes office, he or she must organize the advisors.
   g. The server spilled soup all over her boss.
   h. The boss asked if she would be willing to work on the phone lines.
   i. To become a police officer, you need considerable training.
   j. Has the mail carrier arrived yet?

U7 Active and Passive Voice

1. page 51
   a. The board of governors raises funds for special events at the Royal Botanical Gardens.
   b. A demure, young woman named Phoebe represented the radical faction of the party.

- c. The company's negotiating team made grave mistakes at this year's salary meeting.
- d. In the hit TV show *24*, Canadian actor Kiefer Sutherland plays Jack Bauer.
- e. The topic sentence concisely conveys the paragraph's subject.
- f. The new anti-smoking legislation alarmed the tobacco companies.
- g. At the national boxing championships, a newcomer knocked out the former champion in the fifth round.
- h. A lot of high schoolers experience a disappointing prom night every June.
- i. Canadians offered millions of dollars in aid to the South Asian countries affected by the tsunami disaster.
- j. A rival firm offered the construction engineer a new position.

2. page 52
- a. The company's income statement clearly shows that employees were poorly paid for their labour.
- b. The students submitted all the assignments on the final day of classes.
- c. Nortel Communications released a new set of financial statements.
- d. Dr. Fong diagnosed her condition as chronic fatigue syndrome.
- e. Pilot error brought about by fatigue caused the airplane crash.
- f. The latest study of Hitchcock's work corrects many misconceptions about the films.
- g. Everybody who enjoyed the first *Spider-Man* saw *Spider-Man 2*.
- h. Cassius Clay knocked out Sonny Liston in the first round in February, 1964.
- i. The spy used an MP3 player to store the files he downloaded from the company's server.
- j. Ruffians overtook the crowd at the AA hockey game.

PUNCTUATION

P1 The Comma

1. page 53
- a. Correct
- b. Sri Lanka, Thailand, and Indonesia suffered immense devastation and loss of life when a tsunami struck the Indian Ocean.
- c. Correct
- d. Correct
- e. The lights were lowered, and a quiet hush descended over the audience.
- f. Regardless of how much money you want to make, you have to make it ethically.
- g. Whenever they sat down to eat, the baby started screaming.
- h. Correct
- i. If you had listened to me in the first place, this disaster would not have happened.
- j. Bryan Adams, best known as one of the most popular Canadian rock singers and performers, is now considered one of the best portrait photographers in the world.

2. page 54
   a. As she answered the door, Jamie Lee thought of all the horror movies she had seen in her life.
   b. There is, in fact, no evidence to support the charges of corruption against the city councillor.
   c. Instead of drinking wine, I now imbibe club soda.
   d. The pearls in the garage sale were sold immediately, but she hadn't meant to put them out with the costume jewellery.
   e. Yes, there are a number of ways to sell your products online.
   f. Mr. Deeds, you don't realize what you are asking!
   g. I cannot understand how, in a world so reliant on technology, she can live without having a telephone.
   h. What your mother thinks of my apartment doesn't concern me.
   i. Jason was about to take a shower after his workout but changed his mind.
   j. Good manners suggest, therefore, that you use your napkin to wipe your hands.

P2 and P3 The Semicolon and the Colon

1. page 55
   a. Mary's grocery list always included cat food and magazines.
   b. The contributions came from Canada, the USA, France, Germany and England.
   c. Correct
   d. Marian was shocked when Li told everyone she had she'd failed the chemistry mid-term; she thought she could trust Li to keep a secret.
   e. The coaches' advice proved correct; the team played better than ever but still lost.
   f. The campers could not stand the weather, which was no wonder because the air was cold, and the mosquitoes were troublesome.
   g. Ansel decided to take pictures only of landscapes: dramatic, unique, colourful landscapes.
   h. Correct
   i. Dennis tried everything to get her attention, including shouting and running back and forth.
   j. Nancy wore gumboots, a slicker, and her warmest mittens.

P3 Review of the Semicolon, the Colon, and the Comma

1. page 56

   The way of life for many Canadians is changing[,] but does anybody know what that really means? In Saskatchewan[,] for example[,] farmers have been abandoning their land in droves over the past ten years. In 1990[,] rural municipalities accounted for 20 percent of Saskatchewan's population[;] by the end of the decade[,] however[,] they were only 15 percent. Numbers[,] of course[,] tell only part of the story. People are moving away from the rural areas to cities like Calgary and Edmonton[,] and the small towns that serviced them are shrinking and dying. In just another decade places such as Mendham[,] Eastend[,] and Swift Current will be completely unpopulated. Houses will stand empty[,] and stores[,] businesses[,] and churches that once bustled with people will have locked their doors permanently. The prairie towns are disappearing and are taking with them a part of Canada's heritage.

2. page 56
Residents of the town of Mendham[,] Saskatchewan[,] have one piece of advice for anyone wanting to pay their town a visit[:] Hurry up before its gone! This is because the town's population has been decreasing rapidly over the past decade[;] in a few years[,] it may become only a name on the map of southern Saskatchewan. However[,] life in Mendham has not always been this way. The town was once a centre of activity and boasted the following[:] a bowling alley[,] a pool hall[,] five service stations[,] a lumberyard[,] a car dealership[,] three churches[,] and three grocery stores. There is[,] perhaps[,] no better illustration of the decline of rural life than the field on the outskirts of the town[;] on it lie the rusting remains of dozens of tractors. These machines[,] once a vital part of the area's livelihood[,] are themselves now harvested for their spare parts.

3. page 57
Small town life across Canada is permanently changing. Often[ ] however[ ] the forces of change are government policy instead of economic factors. Half a century ago[ ] there were about 1[ ]200 settlements in Newfoundland. The inhabitants of these tiny villages fished the ocean for their livelihood[ ] and many of them built the houses they lived in. The towns had names as colourful as some of the characters that lived in them. For example[,] have you ever heard of Ireland's Eye[,] Indian Burying Place[,] or Great Paradise? The harsh climate and decades of neglect have reduced these towns to piles of rotting lumber.

4. page 57
Along 10[,]000 kilometres of Newfoundland's coastline are the remnants of over a thousand fishing villages. The residents of these towns left their homes not because they could no longer fish the oceans[;] they left because they were paid to leave. Joey Smallwood[,] the premier of Newfoundland at the time[,] had a vision[:] move people from these tiny "outports" to several centres of economic growth. Once there[,] these people would work in modern fisheries or factories that the premier hoped industrialists would erect. Few of these facilities were ever built[;] however[,] for more than forty years, the federal and provincial governments paid more than 28[,]000 people to move from the old settlements. Some were happy to leave the poor conditions in these towns[;] others were more reluctant and felt that they were little more than pieces in a game played by the government.

P5 Apostrophes

1. page 58
    a. The babies' baths were too hot for tender skin.
    b. This candy's taste reminds me of spiced apples.
    c. The police hadn't anticipated the spray's effect before using in on the suspect.
    d. The class's spirit lifted when they discovered they'd be allowed to rewrite the test.

e. Professor Bohrs began every class by reciting the students' names.
f. They say that Saturday's child is full of grace.
g. The three weeks' sale is over.
h. The cat's flea collar was around its neck.
i. The Smiths' party was the best, better even than ours.
j. The Niagara Falls' ride was really thrilling.

2. page 58
   a. The hunters' time is wasted if their luck is bad.
   b. In January, men's and women's coats were on sale for half the regular price.
   c. Its eyes glowed eerily in the moon's waning light.
   d. Bess's dress was a bright blue, which matched her eyes.
   e. We thought the agents' reports were missing until we realized they'd given them to the enemy.
   f. Conrad brought an album of U2's greatest hits to Charles' part on Saturday.
   g. In many large cities, citizens' groups have been formed to prevent crime.
   h. Harry has always loved his mother-in-law's cooking more than his wife's.
   i. Theirs was not a happy home but neither was ours.
   j. Mr. James is waiting for the train sets to go on sale before he'll buy one for his sons.

P5 Other Punctuation Marks

1. page 59
   a. Jim Carrey - perhaps the most famous Canadian actor - lived a life of poverty while growing up in Toronto.
   b. Who knows the poem "My Funny Valentine"?
   c. My son's only two, but he knows the words to "Baa, Baa Black Sheep".
   d. Jason wrote a poem called Water Towers, which was about the industrial neighbourhood he grew up in (now completely transformed by development).
   e. Myron's hobbies - photography and music - are among the most expensive anyone could ever have.
   f. "It's a small price to pay for ensuring happiness and mental health," he often says.
   g. Essential oils (of which Omega 3 is the best-known) are derived mostly from fish - mackerel, shark and especially cod.
   h. Neighbours called him "knucklehead" not because he was stupid (indeed, he had a Ph.D. in astrophysics) but because rode an old Harley-Davidson motorcycle made famous by its knuckle-shaped cylinder heads.
   i. "Do you realize," she said, "how much money we've spent on this car lately?"
   j. Look up the word "irregardless" in the dictionary.

P6 Punctuation Review

1. page 60

Inquiry, as a form of learning, is useful to allow people to find real answers to problems they pose themselves and to learn how to do research—not just in the library, in traditional fashion, but with others through interviews, surveys, and discussion or reflection. Inquiry is useful to survey a field or to allow the creative input of those involved in a particular subject area. The teacher can coach students, but essentially the object is for learners to teach themselves as they go along, with some monitoring from the teacher and assistance from others, perhaps in group situations.

Inquiry is not directed by the teacher but instead by the learner. Students learn to be independent, and they frame questions and solutions for themselves. When all the resources are widely dispersed, inquiry is especially useful to explore new areas. In an inquiry course such as Topics in Multimedia, students work in groups to explore questions about censorship on the Internet and the value of the Internet for education. They learn research skills and find a number of resources not known to any of us before. The nature of Internet research itself leads to this kind of open-ended research, for it helps students find their feet in research situations, in which they need to frame their own answerable clear questions and solutions to them.

2. page 61

Students, as a general rule, use study questions as the basis for their learning, do workshops on Internet research, and learn how to conduct group discussions, which are intended to help them accomplish their goals. We "contract" with each other; that is, we have a schedule of presentations and due dates for final reports when the group will submit one assignment. Participation, on a regular basis, is also an essential part of the contract.

Inquiry teaching does not lead a student through course material; in fact, the students, to a large extent, find their own course material. Courses are in most cases divided into cycles: the students meet in groups to decide on a topic, then they gather information, then they work to synthesize, and finally they present it to the rest of the group and submit a report to the teacher. Students are taught research skills and writing skills; helped to select workable topics; and given guidelines for their presentations and reports.

Inquiry teaching requires a lot of trust: teachers don't go in to class with an agenda or a lecture prepared. They go in with perhaps a small lesson on research methods but, mostly, with an eye to watching over groups as they meet and discuss their topics. Teachers do a lot of monitoring and almost no "front of the class" teaching.

MECHANICS

M2 Capitalization

1. page 62
   a. When Columbus reached the West Indies in 1492, he thought he'd reached India.
   b. The King of France sent Jacques Cartier to what is now Canada in order to find wealth, claim land and explore the Gulf of St. Lawrence.
   c. Joel Bakan's book, *The Corporation: The Pathological Pursuit of Profit and Power,* was a bestseller and was turned into an award-winning documentary.
   d. Florence thought that *The Chicago Manual of Style* was a home decorating book.
   e. Correct
   f. French, Italian and Romanian are all derived from Latin, which was spread throughout the European continent by Roman soldiers over 2,000 years ago.
   g. It is important for professors to understand that their Muslim students will probably experience fatigue in class during Ramadan, the holy month of fasting.
   h. A robotic probe launched from Earth two years ago finally landed on Titan, the largest of Jupiter's moons.
   i. Abu Dubai, which is the Capital City of the United Arab Emirates, is a popular destination for shoppers around the world because no one pays import and export duties.
   j. You can't find anywhere in history a better example of musical genius than the Beach Boys.

M3 Abbreviations

1. page 63
   a. Sitting in the auditorium with hundreds of other students, Janice found her introductory psychchology class intimidating.
   b. The U.S. markets have been plummeting lately.
   c. The U.S. economic indicators do not look very promising these days.
   d. Correct
   e. This year Christmas will fall on a Wednesday.
   f. Worldvision, CARE and UNICEF helped to organize aid to those countries stricken by the earthquake and tsunami in the Indian Ocean.
   g. The doctor who specializes in back injuries examined Mortimer after he fell from the ladder at work.
   h. Despite an improving regional economy, Prince Edward Island will always be Canada's smallest province.
   i. Correct
   j. Canada has many diplomatic connections with the United Kingdom.

M4 Numbers

1. page 64
   a. About four years ago, Martin and Laura had their second child, and after that their lives have never been the same.
   b. Correct
   c. Correct.
   d. I paid $120 to have the brakes on my Italian racing bicycle repaired.
   e. After his third divorce, Tom went to China and started his life over.
   f. With seventy-five students and only one teacher, this class has a 75:1 student-teacher ratio.
   g. Eleven MLAs from some of the most important ridings urged Premier Klein to run for a fourth term in office.
   h. Act I, scene I of *Macbeth* introduces the three witches.
   i. The amount that the Canadian government pledge to relief efforts totalled $425 million.
   j. Correct.

M5 Hyphens

1. page 65
   a. Today is my forty-ninth birthday.
   b. My father thinks he's getting his money's worth if dines at an all-you-can eat buffet.
   c. My brother-in-law was seriously injured when he slipped on a puddle in the grocery store.
   d. Correct
   e. The Lieutenant-Governor and the Governor General attended the opening of the hospital's new wing.
   f. Correct
   g. My Member of Parliament intervened on our behalf to halt construction of the new housing development.
   h. Well-known author and singer, Vic Dane appeared at the Limelight Club on Saturday.
   i. Highly developed self-esteem is something many excellent public speakers possess.
   j. One-fifth of all respondents said that they did not care who ran the offshore oil well.